JUSTICE

BY
JOHN GALSWORTHY

Fredonia Books
Amsterdam, The Netherlands

Justice:
A Tragedy in Four Acts

by
John Galsworthy

ISBN: 1-58963-466-7

Fredonia Books
Amsterdam, the Netherlands
http://www.fredoniabooks.com

JUSTICE

A TRAGEDY IN FOUR ACTS

PERSONS OF THE PLAY

JAMES HOW ⎱ *solicitors*
WALTER HOW, *his son* ⎰

ROBERT COKESON, *their managing clerk*
WILLIAM FALDER, *their junior clerk*
SWEEDLE, *their office-boy*
WISTER, *a detective*
COWLEY, *a cashier*
MR. JUSTICE FLOYD, *a judge*
HAROLD CLEAVER, *an old advocate*
HECTOR FROME, *a young advocate*
CAPTAIN DANSON, V.C., *a prison governor*
THE REV. HUGH MILLER, *a prison chaplain*
EDWARD CLEMENTS, *a prison doctor*
WOODER, *a chief warder*
MOANEY ⎫
CLIPTON ⎬ *convicts*
O'CLEARY ⎭
RUTH HONEYWILL, *a woman*
A NUMBER OF BARRISTERS, SOLICITORS, SPECTATORS,
    USHERS, REPORTERS, JURYMEN, WARDERS, AND
    PRISONERS

TIME: The Present.

CAST OF THE FIRST PRODUCTION

AT THE

DUKE OF YORK'S THEATRE, FEBRUARY 21, 1910

James How	Mr. Sydney Valentine
Walter How	Mr. Charles Maude
Cokeson	Mr. Edmund Gwenn
Falder	Mr. Dennis Eadie
The Office-boy	Mr. George Hersee
The Detective	Mr. Leslie Carter
The Cashier	Mr. C. E. Vernon
The Judge	Mr. Dion Boucicault
The Old Advocate	Mr. Oscar Adye
The Young Advocate	Mr. Charles Bryant
The Prison Governor	Mr. Grendon Bentley
The Prison Chaplain	Mr. Hubert Harben
The Prison Doctor	Mr. Lewis Casson
Wooder	Mr. Frederick Lloyd
Moaney	Mr. Robert Pateman
Clipton	Mr. O. P. Heggie
O'Cleary	Mr. Whitford Kane
Ruth Honeywill	Miss Edyth Olive

ACT I

The scene is the managing clerk's room, at the offices of
JAMES AND WALTER HOW, *on a July morning.*
The room is old-fashioned, furnished with well-worn
mahogany and leather, and lined with tin boxes and
estate plans. It has three doors. Two of them
are close together in the centre of a wall. One of
these two doors leads to the outer office, which is
only divided from the managing clerk's room by a
partition of wood and clear glass; and when the
door into this outer office is opened there can be
seen the wide outer door leading out on to the stone
stairway of the building. The other of these two
centre doors leads to the junior clerk's room. The
third door is that leading to the partners' room.
The managing clerk, COKESON, *is sitting at his table*
adding up figures in a pass-book, and murmuring
their numbers to himself. He is a man of sixty,
wearing spectacles; rather short, with a bald head,
and an honest, pug-dog face. He is dressed in a
well-worn black frock-coat and pepper-and-salt
trousers.

COKESON. And five's twelve, and three—fifteen,
nineteen, twenty-three, thirty-two, forty-one—and carry

1

four. [*He ticks the page, and goes on murmuring*]
Five, seven, twelve, seventeen, twenty-four and nine,
thirty-three, thirteen and carry one.

> *He again makes a tick. The outer office
> door is opened, and* SWEEDLE, *the office-boy,
> appears, closing the door behind him. He
> is a pale youth of sixteen, with spiky hair.*

COKESON. [*With grumpy expectation*] And carry
one.

SWEEDLE. There's a party wants to see Falder, Mr.
Cokeson.

COKESON. Five, nine, sixteen, twenty-one, twenty-
nine—and carry two. Sent him to Morris's. What
name?

SWEEDLE. Honeywill.

COKESON. What's his business?

SWEEDLE. It's a woman.

COKESON. A lady?

SWEEDLE. No, a person.

COKESON. Ask her in. Take this pass-book to
Mr. James. [*He closes the pass-book.*

SWEEDLE. [*Reopening the door*] Will you come in,
please?

> RUTH HONEYWILL *comes in. She is a tall
> woman, twenty-six years old, unpreten-
> tiously dressed, with black hair and eyes,
> and an ivory-white, clear-cut face. She
> stands very still, having a natural dignity of
> pose and gesture.*

SWEEDLE *goes out into the partners' room with the pass-book.*

COKESON. [*Looking round at* RUTH] The young man's out. [*Suspiciously*] State your business, please.

RUTH. [*Who speaks in a matter-of-fact voice, and with a slight West-Country accent*] It's a personal matter, sir.

COKESON. We don't allow private callers here. Will you leave a message?

RUTH. I'd rather see him, please.

She narrows her dark eyes and gives him a honeyed look.

COKESON. [*Expanding*] It's all against the rules. Suppose I had *my* friends here to see me! It'd never do!

RUTH. No, sir.

COKESON. [*A little taken aback*] Exactly! And here you are wanting to see a *junior* clerk!

RUTH. Yes, sir; I must see him.

COKESON. [*Turning full round to her with a sort of outraged interest*] But this is a lawyer's office. Go to his private address.

RUTH. He's not there.

COKESON. [*Uneasy*] Are you related to the party?

RUTH. No, sir.

COKESON. [*In real embarrassment*] I don't know what to say. It's no affair of the office.

RUTH. But what am I to do?

COKESON. Dear me! I can't tell you that.

> SWEEDLE *comes back. He crosses to the outer office and passes through into it, with a quizzical look at* COKESON, *carefully leaving the door an inch or two open.*

COKESON. [*Fortified by this look*] This won't do, you know, this won't do at all. Suppose one of the partners came in!

> *An incoherent knocking and chuckling is heard from the outer door of the outer office.*

SWEEDLE. [*Putting his head in*] There's some children outside here.

RUTH. They're mine, please.

SWEEDLE. Shall I hold them in check?

RUTH. They're quite small, sir. [*She takes a step towards* COKESON.

COKESON. You mustn't take up his time in office hours; we're a clerk short as it is.

RUTH. It's a matter of life and death.

COKESON. [*Again outraged*] Life and death!

SWEEDLE. Here *is* Falder.

> FALDER *has entered through the outer office. He is a pale, good-looking young man, with quick, rather scared eyes. He moves towards the door of the clerks' office, and stands there irresolute.*

COKESON. Well, I'll give you a minute. It's not regular.

> *Taking up a bundle of papers, he goes out into the partners' room.*

RUTH. [*In a low, hurried voice*] He's on the drink again, Will. He tried to cut my throat last night. I came out with the children before he was awake. I went round to you——

FALDER. I've changed my digs.

RUTH. Is it all ready for to-night?

FALDER. I've got the tickets. Meet me 11.45 at the booking office. For God's sake don't forget we're man and wife! [*Looking at her with tragic intensity*] Ruth!

RUTH. You're not afraid of going, are you?

FALDER. Have you got your things, and the children's?

RUTH. Had to leave them, for fear of waking Honeywill, all but one bag. I can't go near home again.

FALDER. [*Wincing*] All that money gone for nothing. How much *must* you have?

RUTH. Six pounds—I could do with that, I think.

FALDER. Don't give away where we're going. [*As if to himself*] When I get out there I mean to forget it all.

RUTH. If you're sorry, say so. I'd sooner he killed me than take you against your will.

FALDER. [*With a queer smile*] We've *got* to go. I don't care; I'll have *you*.

RUTH. You've just to say; it's not too late.

FALDER. It *is* too late. Here's seven pounds. Booking office—11.45 to-night. If you weren't what you are to me, Ruth——!

RUTH. Kiss me!

> *They cling together passionately, then fly apart just as* COKESON *re-enters the room.* RUTH *turns and goes out through the outer office.* COKESON *advances deliberately to his chair and seats himself.*

COKESON. This isn't right, Falder.

FALDER. It shan't occur again, sir.

COKESON. It's an improper use of these premises.

FALDER. Yes, sir.

COKESON. You quite understand—the party was in some distress; and, having children with her, I allowed my feelings—— [*He opens a drawer and produces from it a tract*] Just take this! "Purity in the Home." It's a well-written thing.

FALDER. [*Taking it, with a peculiar expression*] Thank you, sir.

COKESON. And look here, Falder, before Mr. Walter comes, have you finished up that cataloguing Davis had in hand before he left?

FALDER. I shall have done with it to-morrow, sir—for good.

COKESON. It's over a week since Davis went. Now it won't do, Falder. You're neglecting your work for private life. I shan't mention about the party having called, but——

FALDER. [*Passing into his room*] Thank you, sir.

> COKESON *stares at the door through which* FALDER *has gone out; then shakes his head, and is just settling down to write, when*

WALTER *How comes in through the outer*
office. He is a rather refined-looking man
of thirty-five, with a pleasant, almost apolo-
getic voice.

WALTER. Good-morning, Cokeson.

COKESON. Morning, Mr. Walter.

WALTER. My father here?

COKESON. [*Always with a certain patronage as to a*
young man who might be doing better] Mr. James has
been here since eleven o'clock.

WALTER. I've been in to see the pictures, at the
Guildhall.

COKESON. [*Looking at him as though this were*
exactly what was to be expected] Have you now—ye-es.
This lease of Boulter's—am I to send it to counsel?

WALTER. What does my father say?

COKESON. 'Aven't bothered him.

WALTER. Well, we can't be too careful.

COKESON. It's such a little thing—hardly worth
the fees. I thought you'd do it yourself.

WALTER. Send it, please. I don't want the responsibility.

COKESON. [*With an indescribable air of compassion*]
Just as you like. This "right-of-way" case—we've
got 'em on the deeds.

WALTER. I know; but the intention was obviously
to exclude that bit of common ground.

COKESON. We needn't worry about that. We're
the *right* side of the law.

WALTER. I don't like it.

COKESON. [*With an indulgent smile*] We shan't want to set ourselves up against the law. Your father wouldn't waste his time doing that.

> *As he speaks* JAMES HOW *comes in from the partners' room. He is a shortish man, with white side-whiskers, plentiful grey hair, shrewd eyes, and gold pince-nez.*

JAMES. Morning, Walter.

WALTER. How are you, father?

COKESON. [*Looking down his nose at the papers in his hand as though deprecating their size*] I'll just take Boulter's lease in to young Falder to draft the instructions.   [*He goes out into* FALDER'S *room.*

WALTER. About that right-of-way case?

JAMES. Oh, well, we must go forward there. I thought you told me yesterday the firm's balance was over four hundred.

WALTER. So it is.

JAMES. [*Holding out the pass-book to his son*] Three —five—one, no recent cheques. Just get me out the cheque-book.

> WALTER *goes to a cupboard, unlocks a drawer, and produces a cheque-book.*

JAMES. Tick the pounds in the counterfoils. Five, fifty-four, seven, five, twenty-eight, twenty, ninety, eleven, fifty-two, seventy-one. Tally?

WALTER. [*Nodding*] Can't understand. Made sure it was over four hundred.

JAMES. Give me the cheque-book. [*He takes the*

cheque-book and cons the counterfoils] What's this ninety?

WALTER. Who drew it?

JAMES. You.

WALTER. [*Taking the cheque-book*] July 7th? That's the day I went down to look over the Trenton Estate —last Friday week; I came back on the Tuesday, you remember. But look here, father, it was *nine* I drew a cheque for. Five guineas to Smithers and my expenses. It just covered all but half a crown.

JAMES. [*Gravely*] Let's look at that ninety cheque. [*He sorts the cheque out from the bundle in the pocket of the pass-book*] Seems all right. There's no nine here. This is bad. Who cashed that nine-pound cheque?

WALTER. [*Puzzled and pained*] Let's see! I was finishing Mrs. Reddy's will—only just had time; yes —I gave it to Cokeson.

JAMES. Look at that t y : that yours?

WALTER. [*After consideration*] My *y's* curl back a little; this doesn't.

JAMES. [*As* COKESON *re-enters from* FALDER'S *room*] We must ask him. Just come here and carry your mind back a bit, Cokeson. D'you remember cashing a cheque for Mr. Walter last Friday week—the day he went to Trenton?

COKESON. Ye-es. Nine pounds.

JAMES. Look at this.   [*Handing him the cheque.*

COKESON. No! Nine pounds. My lunch was just coming in; and of course I *like* it hot; I gave the cheque to Davis to run round to the bank. He brought it back, all gold—you remember, Mr. Walter, you wanted some silver to pay your cab. [*With a certain contemptuous compassion*] Here, let *me* see. You've got the wrong cheque.

> He takes cheque-book and pass-book from WALTER.

WALTER. Afraid not.

COKESON. [*Having seen for himself*] It's funny.

JAMES. You gave it to Davis, and Davis sailed for Australia on Monday. Looks black, Cokeson.

COKESON. [*Puzzled and upset*] Why this'd be a felony! No, no! there's some mistake.

JAMES. I hope so.

COKESON. There's never been anything of that sort in the office the twenty-nine years I've been here.

JAMES. [*Looking at cheque and counterfoil*] This is a very clever bit of work; a warning to you not to leave space after your figures, Walter.

WALTER. [*Vexed*] Yes, I know—I was in such a tearing hurry that afternoon.

COKESON. [*Suddenly*] This has upset me.

JAMES. The counterfoil altered too—very deliberate piece of swindling. What was Davis's ship?

WALTER. *City of Rangoon.*

JAMES. We ought to wire and have him arrested at Naples; he can't be there yet.

COKESON. His poor young wife. I liked the young man. Dear, oh dear! In this office!

WALTER. Shall I go to the bank and ask the cashier?

JAMES. [*Grimly*] Bring him round here. And ring up Scotland Yard.

WALTER. Really?

> *He goes out through the outer office.* JAMES *paces the room. He stops and looks at* COKESON, *who is disconsolately rubbing the knees of his trousers.*

JAMES. Well, Cokeson! There's something in character, isn't there?

COKESON. [*Looking at him over his spectacles*] I don't quite take you, sir.

JAMES. Your story would sound d——d thin to any one who didn't know you.

COKESON. Ye-es! [*He laughs. Then with sudden gravity*] I'm sorry for that young man. I feel it as if it was my own son, Mr. James.

JAMES. A nasty business!

COKESON. It unsettles you. All goes on regular, and then a thing like this happens. Shan't relish my lunch to-day.

JAMES. As bad as that, Cokeson?

COKESON. It makes you think. [*Confidentially*] He must have had temptation.

JAMES. Not so fast. We haven't convicted him yet.

COKESON. I'd sooner have lost a month's salary than had this happen.   [*He broods.*

JAMES. I hope that fellow will hurry up.

COKESON. [*Keeping things pleasant for the cashier*] It isn't fifty yards, Mr. James   He won't be a minute.

JAMES. The idea of dishonesty about this office—
it hits me hard, Cokeson.

    He goes towards the door of the partners' room.

SWEEDLE. [*Entering quietly, to* COKESON *in a low voice*] She's popped up again, sir—something she forgot to say to Falder.

COKESON. [*Roused from his abstraction*] Eh? Impossible. Send her away!

JAMES. What's that?

COKESON. Nothing, Mr. James. A private matter. Here, I'll come myself. [*He goes into the outer office as* JAMES *passes into the partners' room*] Now, you really mustn't—we can't have anybody just now.

RUTH. Not for a minute, sir?

COKESON. Reely! Reely! I can't have it. If you want him, wait about; he'll be going out for his lunch directly.

RUTH. Yes, sir.

    WALTER, *entering with the cashier, passes*
        RUTH *as she leaves the outer office.*

COKESON. [*To the cashier, who resembles a sedentary dragoon*] Good-morning. [To WALTER] Your father's in there.

    WALTER *crosses and goes into the partners'*
        room.

COKESON. It's a nahsty, unpleasant little matter, Mr. Cowley. I'm quite ashamed to have to trouble you.

COWLEY. I remember the cheque quite well. [*As if it were a liver*] Seemed in perfect order.

COKESON. Sit down, won't you? I'm not a sensitive man, but a thing like this about the place—it's not nice. I like people to be open and jolly together.

COWLEY. Quite so.

COKESON. [*Buttonholing him, and glancing towards the partners' room*] Of course he's a young man. I've told him about it before now—leaving space after his figures, but he *will* do it.

COWLEY. I should remember the person's face—quite a youth.

COKESON. I don't think we shall be able to show him to you, as a matter of fact.

> JAMES *and* WALTER *have come back from the partners' room.*

JAMES. Good-morning, Mr. Cowley. You've seen my son and myself, you've seen Mr. Cokeson, and you've seen Sweedle, my office-boy. It was none of us, I take it.

> *The cashier shakes his head with a smile.*

JAMES. Be so good as to sit there. Cokeson, engage Mr. Cowley in conversation, will you?

> *He goes towards* FALDER'S *room.*

COKESON. Just a word, Mr. James.

JAMES. Well?

COKESON. You don't want to upset the young man in there, do you? He's a nervous young feller.

JAMES. This must be thoroughly cleared up, Cokeson, for the sake of Falder's name, to say nothing of yours.

COKESON. [*With some dignity*] That'll look after

itself, sir. He's been upset once this morning; I don't want him startled again.

JAMES. It's a matter of form; but I can't stand upon niceness over a thing like this—too serious. Just talk to Mr. Cowley.

> *He opens the door of* FALDER'S *room.*

JAMES. Bring in the papers in Boulter's lease, will you, Falder?

COKESON. [*Bursting into voice*] Do you keep dogs?

> *The cashier, with his eyes fixed on the door, does not answer.*

COKESON. You haven't such a thing as a bulldog pup you could spare me, I suppose?

> *At the look on the cashier's face his jaw drops, and he turns to see* FALDER *standing in the doorway, with his eyes fixed on* COWLEY, *like the eyes of a rabbit fastened on a snake.*

FALDER. [*Advancing with the papers*] Here they are, sir!

JAMES. [*Taking them*] Thank you.

FALDER. Do you want me, sir?

JAMES. No, thanks!

> FALDER *turns and goes back into his own room. As he shuts the door* JAMES *gives the cashier an interrogative look, and the cashier nods.*

JAMES. Sure? This isn't as we suspected.

COWLEY. Quite. He knew me. I suppose he can't slip out of that room?

COKESON. [*Gloomily*] There's only the window—a whole floor and a basement.

> *The door of* FALDER'S *room is quietly opened, and* FALDER, *with his hat in his hand, moves towards the door of the outer office.*

JAMES. [*Quietly*] Where are you going, Falder?

FALDER. To have my lunch, sir.

JAMES. Wait a few minutes, would you? I want to speak to you about this lease.

FALDER. Yes, sir.   [*He goes back into his room.*

COWLEY. If I'm wanted, I can swear that's the young man who cashed the cheque. It was the last cheque I handled that morning before my lunch. These are the numbers of the notes he had. [*He puts a slip of paper on the table; then, brushing his hat round*] Good-morning!

JAMES. Good-morning, Mr. Cowley!

COWLEY. [*To* COKESON] Good-morning.

COKESON. [*With stupefaction*] Good-morning.

> *The cashier goes out through the outer office.* COKESON *sits down in his chair, as though it were the only place left in the morass of his feelings.*

WALTER. What are you going to do?

JAMES. Have him in. Give me the cheque and the counterfoil.

COKESON. I don't understand. I thought young Davis——

JAMES. We shall see.

WALTER. One moment, father: have you thought it out?

JAMES. Call him in!

COKESON. [*Rising with difficulty and opening* FAL-DER'S *door; hoarsely*] Step in here a minute.

FALDER *comes in.*

FALDER. [*Impassively*] Yes, sir?

JAMES. [*Turning to him suddenly with the cheque held out*] You know this cheque, Falder?

FALDER. No, sir.

JAMES. Look at it.   You cashed it last Friday week.

FALDER. Oh! yes, sir; that one—Davis gave it me.

JAMES. I know.   And you gave Davis the cash?

FALDER. Yes, sir.

JAMES. When Davis gave you the cheque was it exactly like this?

FALDER. Yes, I think so, sir.

JAMES. You know that Mr. Walter drew that cheque for *nine* pounds?

FALDER. No, sir—ninety.

JAMES. Nine, Falder.

FALDER. [*Faintly*] I don't understand, sir.

JAMES. The suggestion, of course, is that the cheque was altered; whether by you or Davis is the question.

FALDER. I—I——

COKESON. Take your time, take your time.

FALDER. [*Regaining his impassivity*] Not by me, sir.

JAMES. The cheque was handed to Cokeson by Mr. Walter at one o'clock; we know that because Mr. Cokeson's lunch had just arrived.

COKESON. I couldn't leave it.

JAMES. Exactly; he therefore gave the cheque to Davis. It was cashed by you at 1.15. We know that because the cashier recollects it for the last cheque he handled before *his* lunch.

FALDER. Yes, sir, Davis gave it to me because some friends were giving him a farewell luncheon.

JAMES. [*Puzzled*] You accuse Davis, then?

FALDER. I don't know, sir—it's very funny.

> WALTER, *who has come close to his father, says something to him in a low voice.*

JAMES. Davis was not here again after that Saturday, was he?

COKESON. [*Anxious to be of assistance to the young man, and seeing faint signs of their all being jolly once more*] No, he sailed on the Monday.

JAMES. Was he, Falder?

FALDER. [*Very faintly*] No, sir.

JAMES. Very well, then, how do you account for the fact that this nought was added to the nine in the counterfoil on or after *Tuesday?*

COKESON. [*Surprised*] How's that?

> FALDER *gives a sort of lurch; he tries to pull himself together, but he has gone all to pieces.*

JAMES. [*Very grimly*] Out, I'm afraid, Cokeson. The cheque-book remained in Mr. Walter's pocket till he came back from Trenton on Tuesday morning. In the face of this, Falder, do you still deny that you altered both cheque and counterfoil?

FALDER. No, sir—no, Mr. How. I did it, sir; I did it.

COKESON. [*Succumbing to his feelings*] Dear, dear! what a thing to do!

FALDER. I wanted the money so badly, sir. I didn't know what I was doing.

COKESON. However such a thing could have come into your head!

FALDER. [*Grasping at the words*] I can't think, sir, really! It was just a minute of madness.

JAMES. A long minute, Falder. [*Tapping the counterfoil*] Four days at least.

FALDER. Sir, I swear I didn't know what I'd done till afterwards, and then I hadn't the pluck. Oh! sir, look over it! I'll pay the money back—I will, I promise.

JAMES. Go into your room.

> FALDER, *with a swift imploring look, goes back into his room. There is silence.*

JAMES. About as bad a case as there could be.

COKESON. To break the law like that—in here!

WALTER. What's to be done?

JAMES. Nothing for it. Prosecute.

WALTER. It's his first offence.

JAMES. [*Shaking his head*] I've grave doubts of that. Too neat a piece of swindling altogether.

COKESON. I shouldn't be surprised if he was tempted.

JAMES. Life's one long temptation, Cokeson.

COKESON. Ye-es, but I'm speaking of the flesh

and the devil, Mr. James.   There was a woman come
to see him this morning.

WALTER. The woman we passed as we came in
just now.   Is it his wife?

COKESON. No, no relation. [*Restraining what in
jollier circumstances would have been a wink*] A married
person, though.

WALTER. How do you know?

COKESON. Brought her children. [*Scandalised*]
There they were outside the office.

JAMES. A real bad egg.

WALTER. I should like to give him a chance.

JAMES. I can't forgive him for the sneaky way he
went to work—counting on our suspecting young
Davis if the matter came to light.   It was the merest
accident the cheque-book stayed in your pocket.

WALTER. It *must* have been the temptation of a
moment.   He hadn't time.

JAMES. A man doesn't succumb like that in a moment,
if he's a clean mind and habits.   He's rotten; got the
eyes of a man who can't keep his hands off when there's
money about.

WALTER. [*Dryly*] We hadn't noticed that before.

JAMES. [*Brushing the remark aside*] I've seen lots
of those fellows in my time.   No doing anything with
them except to keep 'em out of harm's way.   They've
got a blind spot.

WALTER. It's penal servitude.

COKESON. They're *nahsty* places—prisons.

JAMES. [*Hesitating*] I don't see how it's possible

to spare him. Out of the question to keep him in this office—honesty's the *sine qua non.*

COKESON. [*Hypnotised*] Of course it *is.*

JAMES. Equally out of the question to send him out amongst people who've no knowledge of his character. One must think of society.

WALTER. But to brand him like this?

JAMES. If it had been a straightforward case I'd give him another chance. It's far from that. He has dissolute habits.

COKESON. I didn't say that—extenuating circumstances.

JAMES. Same thing. He's gone to work in the most cold-blooded way to defraud his employers, and cast the blame on an innocent man. If that's not a case for the law to take its course, I don't know what is.

WALTER. For the sake of his future, though.

JAMES. [*Sarcastically*] According to you, no one would ever prosecute.

WALTER. [*Nettled*] I hate the idea of it.

COKESON. That's *rather ex parte*, Mr. Walter! We must have protection.

JAMES. This is degenerating into talk.

                    He moves towards the partners' room.

WALTER. Put yourself in his place, father.

JAMES. You ask too much of me.

WALTER. We can't possibly tell the pressure there was on him.

JAMES. You may depend on it, my boy, if a man is

going to do this sort of thing he'll do it, pressure or no pressure; if he isn't nothing'll make him.

WALTER. He'll never do it again.

COKESON. [*Fatuously*] S'pose I were to have a talk with him. We don't want to be hard on the young man.

JAMES. That'll do, Cokeson. I've made up my mind.   [*He passes into the partners' room.*

COKESON. [*After a doubtful moment*] We must excuse your father. I don't want to go against your father; if he thinks it right.

WALTER. Confound it, Cokeson! why don't you back me up? You know you feel——

COKESON. [*On his dignity*] I really can't say what I feel.

WALTER. We shall regret it.

COKESON. He must have known what he was doing.

WALTER. [*Bitterly*] "The quality of mercy is not strained."

COKESON. [*Looking at him askance*] Come, come, Mr. Walter. We must try and see it sensible.

SWEEDLE. [*Entering with a tray*] Your lunch, sir.

COKESON. Put it down!

> *While* SWEEDLE *is putting it down on* COKE-
> SON's *table, the detective,* WISTER, *enters the
> outer office, and, finding no one there, comes
> to the inner doorway. He is a square,
> medium-sized man, clean-shaved, in a ser-
> viceable blue serge suit and strong boots.*

WISTER. [*To* WALTER] From Scotland Yard, sir. Detective-Sergeant Wister.

WALTER. [*Askance*] Very well! I'll speak to my father.

> *He goes into the partners' room.* JAMES *enters.*

JAMES. Morning! [*In answer to an appealing gesture from* COKESON] I'm sorry; I'd stop short of this if I felt I could. Open that door. [SWEEDLE, *wondering and scared, opens it*] Come here, Mr. Falder.

> *As* FALDER *comes shrinkingly out, the detective,*
> *in obedience to a sign from* JAMES, *slips his*
> *hand out and grasps his arm.*

FALDER. [*Recoiling*] Oh! no,—oh! no!

WISTER. Come, come, there's a good lad.

JAMES. I charge him with felony.

FALDER. Oh, sir! There's some one—I did it for her. Let me be till to-morrow.

> JAMES *motions with his hand. At that sign of*
> *hardness,* FALDER *becomes rigid. Then,*
> *turning, he goes out quietly in the detective's*
> *grip.* JAMES *follows, stiff and erect.* SWEE-
> DLE, *rushing to the door with open mouth,*
> *pursues them through the outer office into the*
> *corridor. When they have all disappeared*
> COKESON *spins completely round and makes*
> *a rush for the outer office.*

COKESON. [*Hoarsely*] Here! Here! What are we doing?

There is silence. He takes out his handkerchief and mops the sweat from his face. Going back blindly to his table, sits down, and stares blankly at his lunch.

The curtain falls.

ACT II

*A Court of Justice, on a foggy October afternoon—
crowded with barristers, solicitors, reporters, ushers,
and jurymen. Sitting in the large, solid dock is
FALDER, with a warder on either side of him, placed
there for his safe custody, but seemingly indifferent
to and unconscious of his presence. FALDER is
sitting exactly opposite to the JUDGE, who, raised
above the clamour of the court, also seems unconscious
of and indifferent to everything. HAROLD CLEAVER,
the counsel for the Crown, is a dried, yellowish
man, of more than middle age, in a wig worn almost
to the colour of his face. HECTOR FROME, the
counsel for the defence, is a young, tall man, clean-
shaved, in a very white wig. Among the spectators,
having already given their evidence, are JAMES and
WALTER HOW, and COWLEY, the cashier. WISTER,
the detective, is just leaving the witness-box.*

CLEAVER. That is the case for the Crown, me lud!
　　　　　Gathering his robes together, he sits down.
FROME. [*Rising and bowing to the* JUDGE] If it please
your lordship and gentlemen of the jury. I am not
going to dispute the fact that the prisoner altered

25

this cheque, but I am going to put before you evidence
as to the condition of his mind, and to submit that
you would not be justified in finding that he was
responsible for his actions at the time. I am going
to show you, in fact, that he did this in a moment
of aberration, amounting to temporary insanity, caused
by the violent distress under which he was labouring.
Gentlemen, the prisoner is only twenty-three years old.
I shall call before you a woman from whom you will
learn the events that led up to this act. You will hear
from her own lips the tragic circumstances of her life,
the still more tragic infatuation with which she has
inspired the prisoner. This woman, gentlemen, has
been leading a miserable existence with a husband who
habitually ill-uses her, from whom she actually goes in
terror of her life. I am not, of course, saying that it's
either right or desirable for a young man to fall in love
with a married woman, or that it's his business to rescue
her from an ogre-like husband. I'm not saying anything of the sort. But we all know the power of the
passion of love; and I would ask you to remember,
gentlemen, in listening to her evidence, that, married
to a drunken and violent husband, she has no power
to get rid of him; for, as you know, another offence
besides violence is necessary to enable a woman to
obtain a divorce; and of this offence it does not appear
that her husband is guilty.

JUDGE. Is this relevant, Mr. Frome?

FROME. My lord, I submit, extremely—I shall be
able to show your lordship that directly.

JUDGE. Very well.

FROME. In these circumstances, what alternatives were left to her? She could either go on living with this drunkard, in terror of her life; or she could apply to the Court for a separation order. Well, gentlemen, my experience of such cases assures me that this would have given her very insufficient protection from the violence of such a man; and even if effectual would very likely have reduced her either to the workhouse or the streets—for it's not easy, as she is now finding, for an unskilled woman without means of livelihood to support herself and her children without resorting either to the Poor Law or—to speak quite plainly—to the sale of her body.

JUDGE. You are ranging rather far, Mr. Frome.

FROME. I shall fire point-blank in a minute, my lord.

JUDGE. Let us hope so.

FROME. Now, gentlemen, mark—and this is what I have been leading up to—this woman will tell you, and the prisoner will confirm her, that, confronted with such alternatives, she set her whole hopes on himself, knowing the feeling with which she had inspired him. She saw a way out of her misery by going with him to a new country, where they would both be unknown, and might pass as husband and wife. This was a desperate and, as my friend Mr. Cleaver will no doubt call it, an immoral resolution; but, as a fact, the minds of both of them were constantly turned towards it. One wrong is no excuse for another, and those who are never likely to be faced by such a situation possibly have the right to hold up their hands—as to that I prefer to say nothing. But whatever view you take, gentlemen, of this part of the prisoner's story—whatever opinion you form of the right of these two young people under such circumstances to take the law into their own hands—the fact remains that this young woman in her distress, and this young man, little more than a boy, who was so devotedly attached to her, *did* conceive this—if you like —reprehensible design of going away together. Now, for that, of course, they required money, and—they had none. As to the actual events of the morning of July 7th, on which this cheque was altered, the events on which I rely to prove the defendant's irresponsibility—I shall allow those events to speak for themselves, through the lips of my witnesses. Robert Cokeson. [*He turns, looks round, takes up a sheet of paper, and waits.*]

> COKESON *is summoned into court, and goes into*
> *the witness-box, holding his hat before him.*
> *The oath is administered to him.*

FROME. What is your name?

COKESON. Robert Cokeson.

FROME. Are you managing clerk to the firm of solicitors who employ the prisoner?

COKESON. Ye-es.

FROME. How long had the prisoner been in their employ?

COKESON. Two years. No, I'm wrong there—all but seventeen days.

FROME. Had you him under your eye all that time?

COKESON. Except Sundays and holidays.

FROME. Quite so. Let us hear, please, what you have to say about his general character during those two years.

COKESON. [*Confidentially to the jury, and as if a little surprised at being asked*] He was a nice, pleasant-spoken young man. I'd no fault to find with him— quite the contrary. It was a *great* surprise to me when he did a thing like that.

FROME. Did he ever give you reason to suspect his honesty?

COKESON. No! To have dishonesty in our office, that'd never do.

FROME. I'm sure the jury fully appreciate that, Mr. Cokeson.

COKESON. Every man of business knows that honesty's the sign qua non.

FROME. Do you give him a good character all round, or do you not?

COKESON. [*Turning to the* JUDGE] Certainly. We were all very jolly and pleasant together, until this happened. Quite upset me.

FROME. Now, coming to the morning of the 7th of July, the morning on which the cheque was altered. What have you to say about his demeanour that morning?

COKESON. [*To the jury*] If you ask me, I don't think he was quite compos when he did it.

THE JUDGE. [*Sharply*] Are you suggesting that he was insane?

COKESON. Not compos.

THE JUDGE. A little more precision, please.

FROME. [*Smoothly*] Just tell us, Mr. Cokeson.

COKESON. [*Somewhat outraged*] Well, in my opinion —[*looking at the* JUDGE]—such as it is—he was jumpy at the time. The jury will understand my meaning.

FROME. Will you tell us how you came to that conclusion?

COKESON. Ye-es, I will. I have my lunch in from the restaurant, a chop and a potato—saves time. That day it happened to come just as Mr. Walter How handed me the cheque. Well, I like it hot; so I went into the clerks' office and I handed the cheque to Davis, the other clerk, and told him to get change. I noticed young Falder walking up and down. I said to him: "This is not the Zoological Gardens, Falder."

FROME. Do you remember what he answered?

COKESON. Ye-es: "I wish to God it were!" Struck me as funny.

FROME. Did you notice anything else peculiar?

COKESON. I did.

FROME. What was that?

COKESON. His collar was unbuttoned. Now, I like a young man to be neat. I said to him: "Your collar's unbuttoned."

FROME. And what did he answer?

COKESON. Stared at me. It wasn't nice.

THE JUDGE. Stared at you? Isn't that a very common practice?

COKESON. Ye-es, but it was the look in his eyes. I can't explain my meaning—it was funny.

FROME. Had you ever seen such a look in his eyes before?

COKESON. No. If I had I should have spoken to the partners. We can't have anything eccentric in our profession.

THE JUDGE. Did you speak to them on that occasion?

COKESON. [*Confidentially*] Well, I didn't like to trouble them about prime facey evidence.

FROME. But it made a very distinct impression on your mind?

COKESON. Ye-es. The clerk Davis could have told you the same.

FROME. Quite so. It's very unfortunate that we've not got him here. Now can you tell me of the morning on which the discovery of the forgery was made? That would be the 18th. Did anything happen that morning?

COKESON. [*With his hand to his ear*] I'm a little deaf.

FROME. Was there anything in the course of that morning—I mean before the discovery—that caught your attention?

COKESON. Ye-es—a woman.

THE JUDGE. How is *this* relevant, Mr. Frome?

FROME. I am trying to establish the state of mind in which the prisoner committed this act, my lord.

THE JUDGE. I quite appreciate that. But this was long after the act.

FROME. Yes, my lord, but it contributes to my contention.

THE JUDGE. Well!

FROME. You say a woman. Do you mean that she came to the office?

COKESON. Ye-es.

FROME. What for?

COKESON. Asked to see young Falder; he was out at the moment.

FROME. Did you see her?

COKESON. I did.

FROME. Did she come alone?

COKESON. [*Confidentially*] Well, there you put me in a difficulty. I mustn't tell you what the office-boy told me.

FROME. Quite so, Mr. Cokeson, quite so——

COKESON. [*Breaking in with an air of "You are young—leave it to me"*] But I think we can get round it. In answer to a question put to her by a third party the woman said to me: "They're mine, sir."

THE JUDGE. What are? What were?

COKESON. Her children. They were outside.

THE JUDGE. How do you know?

COKESON. Your lordship mustn't ask me that, or I

shall have to tell you what I was told—and that'd never do.

THE JUDGE. [*Smiling*] The office-boy made a statement.

COKESON. Egg-zactly.

FROME. What I want to ask you, Mr. Cokeson, is this. In the course of her appeal to see Falder, did the woman say anything that you specially remember?

COKESON. [*Looking at him as if to encourage him to complete the sentence*] A leetle more, sir.

FROME. Or did she not?

COKESON. She did. I shouldn't like you to have led me to the answer.

FROME. [*With an irritated smile*] Will you tell the jury what it was?

COKESON. "It's a matter of life and death."

FOREMAN OF THE JURY. Do you mean the woman said that?

COKESON. [*Nodding*] It's not the sort of thing you like to have said to you.

FROME. [*A little impatiently*] Did Falder come in while she was there? [COKESON *nods*] And she saw him, and went away?

COKESON. Ah! there I can't follow you. I didn't see her go.

FROME. Well, is she there now?

COKESON. [*With an indulgent smile*] No!

FROME. Thank you, Mr. Cokeson.   [*He sits down.*

CLEAVER. [*Rising*] You say that on the morning of

the forgery the prisoner was jumpy. Well, now, sir, what precisely do you mean by that word?

COKESON. [*Indulgently*] I *want* you to understand. Have you ever seen a dog that's lost its master? He was kind of everywhere at once with his eyes.

CLEAVER. Thank you; I was coming to his eyes. You called them "funny." What are we to understand by that? Strange, or what?

COKESON. Ye-es, funny.

CLEAVER. [*Sharply*] Yes, sir, but what may be funny to you may not be funny to me, or to the jury. Did they look frightened, or shy, or fierce, or what?

COKESON. You make it very hard for me. I give you the word, and you want me to give you another.

CLEAVER. [*Rapping his desk*] Does "funny" mean mad?

COKESON. Not mad, fun——

CLEAVER. Very well! Now you say he had his collar unbuttoned? Was it a hot day?

COKESON. Ye-es; I think it was.

CLEAVER. And did he button it when you called his attention to it?

COKESON. Ye-es, I think he did.

CLEAVER. Would you say that that denoted insanity?

> *He sits down.* COKESON, *who has opened his mouth to reply, is left gaping.*

FROME. [*Rising hastily*] Have you ever caught him in that dishevelled state before?

COKESON. No! He was *always* clean and quiet.

FROME. That will do, thank you.

> COKESON *turns blandly to the* JUDGE, *as though to rebuke counsel for not remembering that the* JUDGE *might wish to have a chance; arriving at the conclusion that he is to be asked nothing further, he turns and descends from the box, and sits down next to* JAMES *and* WALTER.

FROME. Ruth Honeywill.

> RUTH *comes into court, and takes her stand stoically in the witness-box. She is sworn.*

FROME. What is your name, please?

RUTH. Ruth Honeywill.

FROME. How old are you?

RUTH. Twenty-six.

FROME. You are a married woman, living with your husband? A little louder.

RUTH. No, sir; not since July.

FROME. Have you any children?

RUTH. Yes, sir, two.

FROME. Are they living with you?

RUTH. Yes, sir.

FROME. You know the prisoner?

RUTH. [*Looking at him*] Yes.

FROME. What was the nature of your relations with him?

RUTH. We were friends.

THE JUDGE. Friends?

RUTH. [*Simply*] Lovers, sir.

THE JUDGE. [*Sharply*] In what sense do you use that word?

RUTH. We love each other.

THE JUDGE. Yes, but——

RUTH. [*Shaking her head*] No, your lordship—not yet.

THE JUDGE. Not yet! H'm! [*He looks from* RUTH *to* FALDER] Well!

FROME. What is your husband?

RUTH. Traveller.

FROME. And what was the nature of your married life?

RUTH. [*Shaking her head*] It don't bear talking about.

FROME. Did he ill-treat you, or what?

RUTH. Ever since my first was born.

FROME. In what way?

RUTH. I'd rather not say. All sorts of ways.

THE JUDGE. I am afraid I must stop this, you know.

RUTH. [*Pointing to* FALDER] *He* offered to take me out of it, sir. We were going to South America.

FROME. [*Hastily*] Yes, quite—and what prevented you?

RUTH. I was outside his office when he was taken away. It nearly broke my heart.

FROME. You knew, then, that he had been arrested?

RUTH. Yes, sir. I called at his office afterwards, and [*pointing to* COKESON] that gentleman told me all about it.

FROME. Now, do you remember the morning of Friday, July 7th?

RUTH. Yes.

FROME. Why?

RUTH. My husband nearly strangled me that morning.

THE JUDGE. Nearly strangled you!

RUTH. [*Bowing her head*] Yes, my lord.

FROME. With his hands, or——?

RUTH. Yes, I just managed to get away from him. I went straight to my friend. It was eight o'clock.

THE JUDGE. In the morning? Your husband was not under the influence of liquor then?

RUTH. It wasn't always that.

FROME. In what condition were you?

RUTH. In very bad condition, sir. My dress was torn, and I was half choking.

FROME. Did you tell your friend what had happened?

RUTH. Yes. I wish I never had.

FROME. It upset him?

RUTH. Dreadfully.

FROME. Did he ever speak to you about a cheque?

RUTH. Never.

FROME. Did he ever give you any money?

RUTH. Yes.

FROME. When was that?

RUTH. On Saturday.

FROME. The 8th?

RUTH. To buy an outfit for me and the children, and get all ready to start.

FROME. Did that surprise you, or not?

RUTH. What, sir?

FROME. That he had money to give you.

RUTH. Yes, because on the morning when my husband nearly killed me my friend cried because he hadn't the money to get me away. He told me afterwards he'd come into a windfall.

FROME. And when did you last see him?

RUTH. The day he was taken away, sir. It was the day we were to have started.

FROME. Oh, yes, the morning of the arrest. Well, did you see him at all between the Friday and that morning? [RUTH *nods*] What was his manner then?

RUTH. Dumb-like—sometimes he didn't seem able to say a word.

FROME. As if something unusual had happened to him?

RUTH. Yes.

FROME. Painful, or pleasant, or what?

RUTH. Like a fate hanging over him.

FROME. [*Hesitating*] Tell me, did you love the prisoner very much?

RUTH. [*Bowing her head*] Yes.

FROME. And had he a very great affection for you?

RUTH. [*Looking at* FALDER] Yes, sir.

FROME. Now, ma'am, do you or do you not think that your danger and unhappiness would seriously affect his balance, his control over his actions?

RUTH. Yes.

FROME. His reason, even?

RUTH. For a moment like, I think it would.

FROME. Was he very much upset that Friday morning, or was he fairly calm?

RUTH. Dreadfully upset. I could hardly bear to let him go from me.

FROME. Do you still love him?

RUTH. [*With her eyes on* FALDER] He's ruined himself for me.

FROME. Thank you.

> *He sits down.* RUTH *remains stoically upright in the witness-box.*

CLEAVER. [*In a considerate voice*] When you left him on the morning of Friday the 7th you would not say that he was out of his mind, I suppose?

RUTH. No, sir.

CLEAVER. Thank you; I've no further questions to ask you.

RUTH. [*Bending a little forward to the jury*] I would have done the same for him; I would indeed.

THE JUDGE. Please, please! You say your married life is an unhappy one? Faults on both sides?

RUTH. Only that I never bowed down to him. I don't see why I should, sir, not to a man like that.

THE JUDGE. You refused to obey him?

RUTH. [*Avoiding the question*] I've always studied him to keep things nice.

THE JUDGE. Until you met the prisoner—was that it?

RUTH. No; even after that.

THE JUDGE. I ask, you know, because you seem to me to glory in this affection of yours for the prisoner.

RUTH. [*Hesitating*] I—I do. It's the only thing in my life now.

THE JUDGE. [*Staring at her hard*] Well, step down, please.

> RUTH *looks at* FALDER, *then passes quietly down and takes her seat among the witnesses.*

FROME. I call the prisoner, my lord.

> FALDER *leaves the dock; goes into the witness-box, and is duly sworn.*

FROME. What is your name?

FALDER. William Falder.

FROME. And age?

FALDER. Twenty-three.

FROME. You are not married?

> FALDER *shakes his head.*

FROME. How long have you known the last witness?

FALDER. Six months.

FROME. Is her account of the relationship between you a correct one?

FALDER. Yes.

FROME. You became devotedly attached to her, however?

FALDER. Yes.

THE JUDGE. Though you knew she was a married woman?

FALDER. I couldn't help it, your lordship.

THE JUDGE. Couldn't help it?

FALDER. I didn't seem able to.

      The JUDGE *slightly shrugs his shoulders.*

FROME. How did you come to know her?

FALDER. Through my married sister.

FROME. Did you know whether she was happy with her husband?

FALDER. It was trouble all the time.

FROME. You knew her husband?

FALDER. Only through her—he's a brute.

THE JUDGE. I can't allow indiscriminate abuse of a person not present.

FROME. [*Bowing*] If your lordship pleases. [*To* FALDER] You admit altering this cheque?

      FALDER *bows his head.*

FROME. Carry your mind, please, to the morning of Friday, July the 7th, and tell the jury what happened.

FALDER. [*Turning to the jury*] I was having my breakfast when she came. Her dress was all torn, and she was gasping and couldn't seem to get her breath at all; there were the marks of his fingers round her throat; her arm was bruised, and the blood had got into her eyes dreadfully. It frightened me, and then when she told me, I felt—I felt—well—it was too much for me! [*Hardening suddenly*] If you'd seen it, having the feelings for her that I had, you'd have felt the same, I know.

FROME. Yes?

FALDER. When she left me—because I had to go to the office—I was out of my senses for fear that he'd do it again, and thinking what I could do. I

couldn't work—all the morning I was like that—
simply couldn't fix my mind on anything. I couldn't
think at all. I seemed to have to keep moving. When
Davis—the other clerk—gave me the cheque—he said:
"It'll do you good, Will, to have a run with this.
You seem half off your chump this morning." Then
when I had it in my hand—I don't know how it came,
but it just flashed across me that if I put the t y and
the nought there would be the money to get her away.
It just came and went—I never thought of it again.
Then Davis went out to his luncheon, and I don't
really remember what I did till I'd pushed the cheque
through to the cashier under the rail. I remember
his saying "Gold or notes?" Then I suppose I knew
what I'd done. Anyway, when I got outside I wanted
to chuck myself under a 'bus; I wanted to throw the
money away; but it seemed I was in for it, so I thought
at any rate I'd save her. Of course the tickets I took
for the passage and the little I gave her's been wasted,
and all, except what I was obliged to spend myself, I've
restored. I keep thinking over and over however it was
I came to do it, and how I can't have it all again to do
differently!

> FALDER *is silent, twisting his hands before
> him.*

FROME. How far is it from your office to the bank?

FALDER. Not more than fifty yards, sir.

FROME. From the time Davis went out to lunch to
the time you cashed the cheque, how long do you say
it must have been?

FALDER. It couldn't have been four minutes, sir, because I ran all the way.

FROME. During those four minutes you say you remember nothing?

FALDER. No, sir; only that I ran.

FROME. Not even adding the t y and the nought?

FALDER. No, sir. I don't really.

> FROME *sits down, and* CLEAVER *rises.*

CLEAVER. But you remember running, do you?

FALDER. I was all out of breath when I got to the bank.

CLEAVER. And you don't remember altering the cheque?

FALDER. [*Faintly*] No, sir.

CLEAVER. Divested of the romantic glamour which my friend is casting over the case, is this anything but an ordinary forgery? Come.

FALDER. I was half frantic all that morning, sir.

CLEAVER. Now, now! You don't deny that the t y and the nought were so like the rest of the handwriting as to thoroughly deceive the cashier?

FALDER. It was an accident.

CLEAVER. [*Cheerfully*] Queer sort of accident, wasn't it? On which day did you alter the counterfoil?

FALDER. [*Hanging his head*] On the Wednesday morning.

CLEAVER. Was that an accident too?

FALDER. [*Faintly*] No.

CLEAVER. To do that you had to watch your opportunity, I suppose?

FALDER. [*Almost inaudibly*] Yes.

CLEAVER. You don't suggest that you were suffering under great excitement when you did that?

FALDER. I was haunted.

CLEAVER. With the fear of being found out?

FALDER. [*Very low*] Yes.

THE JUDGE. Didn't it occur to you that the only thing for you to do was to confess to your employers, and restore the money?

FALDER. I was afraid. [*There is silence.*

CLEAVER. You desired, too, no doubt, to complete your design of taking this woman away?

FALDER. When I found I'd done a thing like that, to do it for nothing seemed so dreadful. I might just as well have chucked myself into the river.

CLEAVER. You knew that the clerk Davis was about to leave England—didn't it occur to you when you altered this cheque that suspicion would fall on him?

FALDER. It was all done in a moment. I thought of it afterwards.

CLEAVER. And that didn't lead you to avow what you'd done?

FALDER. [*Sullenly*] I meant to write when I got out there—I would have repaid the money.

THE JUDGE. But in the meantime your innocent fellow clerk might have been prosecuted.

FALDER. I knew he was a long way off, your lordship. I thought there'd be time. I didn't think they'd find it out so soon.

FROME. I might remind your lordship that as Mr. Walter How had the cheque-book in his pocket till after Davis had sailed, if the discovery had been made only one day later Falder himself would have left, and suspicion would have attached to him, and not to Davis, from the beginning.

THE JUDGE. The question is whether the prisoner knew that suspicion would light on himself, and not on Davis. [*To* FALDER *sharply*] Did you know that Mr. Walter How had the cheque-book till after Davis had sailed?

FALDER. I—I—thought—he——

THE JUDGE. Now speak the truth—yes or no!

FALDER. [*Very low*] No, my lord. I had no means of knowing.

THE JUDGE. That disposes of your point, Mr. Frome.

[FROME *bows to the* JUDGE.

CLEAVER. Has any aberration of this nature ever attacked you before?

FALDER. [*Faintly*] No, sir.

CLEAVER. You had recovered sufficiently to go back to your work that afternoon?

FALDER. Yes, I had to take the money back.

CLEAVER. You mean the *nine* pounds. Your wits were sufficiently keen for you to remember that? And you still persist in saying you don't remember altering this cheque.   [*He sits down.*

FALDER. If I hadn't been mad I should never have had the courage.

FROME. [*Rising*] Did you have your lunch before going back?

FALDER. I never ate a thing all day; and at night I couldn't sleep.

FROME. Now, as to the four minutes that elapsed between Davis's going out and your cashing the cheque: do you say that you recollect *nothing* during those four minutes?

FALDER. [*After a moment*] I remember thinking of Mr. Cokeson's face.

FROME. Of Mr. Cokeson's face! Had that any connection with what you were doing?

FALDER. No, sir.

FROME. Was that in the office, before you ran out?

FALDER. Yes, and while I was running.

FROME. And that lasted till the cashier said: "Will you have gold or notes?"

FALDER. Yes, and then I seemed to come to myself —and it was too late.

FROME. Thank you. That closes the evidence for the defence, my lord.

> *The* JUDGE *nods, and* FALDER *goes back to his seat in the dock.*

FROME. [*Gathering up notes*] If it please your lordship —Gentlemen of the Jury,—My friend in cross-examination has shown a disposition to sneer at the defence which has been set up in this case, and I am free to admit that nothing I can say will move you, if the evidence has not already convinced you that the prisoner

committed this act in a moment when to all practical
intents and purposes he was not responsible for his
actions; a moment of such mental and moral vacuity,
arising from the violent emotional agitation under which
he had been suffering, as to amount to temporary
madness. My friend has alluded to the "romantic
glamour" with which I have sought to invest this case.
Gentlemen, I have done nothing of the kind. I have
merely shown you the background of "life"—that
palpitating life which, believe me—whatever my friend
may say—always lies behind the commission of a crime.
Now gentlemen, we live in a highly civilized age,
and the sight of brutal violence disturbs us in a very
strange way, even when we have no personal interest
in the matter. But when we see it inflicted on a
woman whom we love—what then? Just think of
what your own feelings would have been, each of you,
at the prisoner's age; and then look at him. Well!
he is hardly the comfortable, shall we say bucolic, person
likely to contemplate with equanimity marks of gross
violence on a woman to whom he was devotedly attached. Yes, gentlemen, look at him! He has not a
strong face; but neither has he a vicious face. He is just
the sort of man who would easily become the prey of
his emotions. You have heard the description of his
eyes. My friend may laugh at the word "funny"—*I*
think it better describes the peculiar uncanny look of
those who are strained to breaking-point than any other
word which could have been used. I don't pretend,
mind you, that his mental irresponsibility was more

than a flash of darkness, in which all sense of proportion became lost; but I do contend, that, just as a man who destroys himself at such a moment may be, and often is, absolved from the stigma attaching to the crime of self-murder, so he may, and frequently does, commit other crimes while in this irresponsible condition, and that he may as justly be acquitted of criminal intent and treated as a patient. I admit that this is a plea which might well be abused. It is a matter for discretion. But here you have a case in which there is every reason to give the benefit of the doubt. You heard me ask the prisoner what he thought of during those four fatal minutes. What was his answer? "I thought of Mr. Cokeson's face!" Gentlemen, no man could invent an answer like that; it is absolutely stamped with truth. You have seen the great affection (legitimate or not) existing between him and this woman, who came here to give evidence for him at the risk of her life. It is impossible for you to doubt his distress on the morning when he committed this act. We well know what terrible havoc such distress can make in weak and highly nervous people. It was all the work of a moment. The rest has followed, as death follows a stab to the heart, or water drops if you hold up a jug to empty it. Believe me, gentlemen, there is nothing more tragic in life than the utter impossibility of changing what you have done. Once this cheque was altered and presented, the work of four minutes—four mad minutes—the rest has been silence. But in those four minutes the boy before you has slipped through a door, hardly opened, into that great cage which never again quite lets a man go—the cage of the Law. His further acts, his failure to confess, the alteration of the counterfoil, his preparations for flight, are all evidence —not of deliberate and guilty intention when he committed the prime act from which these subsequent acts arose; no—they are merely evidence of the weak character which is clearly enough his misfortune. But is a man to be lost because he is bred and born with a weak character? Gentlemen, men like the prisoner are destroyed daily under our law for want of that human insight which sees them as they are, patients, and not criminals. If the prisoner be found guilty, and treated as though he were a criminal type, he will, as all experience shows, in all probability become one. I beg you not to return a verdict that may thrust him back into prison and brand him for ever. Gentlemen, Justice is a machine that, when some one has once given it the starting push, rolls on of itself. Is this young man to be ground to pieces under this machine for an act which at the worst was one of weakness? Is he to become a member of the luckless crews that man those dark, ill-starred ships called prisons? Is that to be his voyage—from which so few return? Or is he to have another chance, to be still looked on as one who has gone a little astray, but who will come back? I urge you, gentlemen, do not ruin this young man! For, as a result of those four minutes, ruin, utter and irretrievable, stares him in the face. He can be saved now. Imprison him as a criminal, and I affirm to you

that he will be lost. He has neither the face nor the
manner of one who can survive that terrible ordeal.
Weigh in the scales his criminality and the suffering he
has undergone. The latter is ten times heavier already.
He has lain in prison under this charge for more than
two months. Is he likely ever to forget that? Imagine
the anguish of his mind during that time. He has had
his punishment, gentlemen, you may depend. The
rolling of the chariot-wheels of Justice over this boy
began when it was decided to prosecute him. We are
now already at the second stage. If you permit it
to go on to the third I would not give—that for him.

> *He holds up finger and thumb in the form of a
> circle, drops his hand, and sits down.*
> *The jury stir, and consult each other's faces;
> then they turn towards the counsel for the
> Crown, who rises, and, fixing his eyes on a
> spot that seems to give him satisfaction,
> slides them every now and then towards
> the jury.*

CLEAVER. May it please your lordship—[*Rising on
his toes*] Gentlemen of the Jury,—The facts in this
case are not disputed, and the defence, if my friend will
allow me to say so, is so thin that I don't propose to
waste the time of the Court by taking you over the
evidence. The plea is one of temporary insanity.
Well, gentlemen, I daresay it is clearer to me than
it is to you why this rather—what shall we call it?—
bizarre defence has been set up. The alternative would
have been to plead guilty. Now, gentlemen, if the

prisoner had pleaded guilty my friend would have had
to rely on a simple appeal to his lordship. Instead of
that, he has gone into the byways and hedges and found
this—er—peculiar plea, which has enabled him to
show you the proverbial woman, to put her in the box—
to give, in fact, a romantic glow to this affair. I com-
pliment my friend; I think it highly ingenious of him.
By these means, he has—to a certain extent—got round
the Law. He has brought the whole story of motive
and stress out in court, at first hand, in a way that he
would not otherwise have been able to do. But when
you have once grasped that fact, gentlemen, you have
grasped everything. [*With good-humoured contempt*]
For look at this plea of insanity; we can't put it lower
than that. You have heard the woman. She has
every reason to favour the prisoner, but what did she
say? She said that the prisoner was *not* insane when
she left him in the morning. If he were going out of
his mind through distress, that was obviously the moment when insanity would have shown itself. You
have heard the managing clerk, another witness for
the defence. With some difficulty I elicited from him
the admission that the prisoner, though jumpy (a word
that he seemed to think you would understand, gentlemen, and I'm sure I hope you do), was *not* mad
when the cheque was handed to Davis. I agree with
my friend that it's unfortunate that we have not got
Davis here, but the prisoner has told you the words
with which Davis in turn handed him the cheque; he
obviously, therefore, was *not* mad when he received it,

or he would not have remembered those words. The cashier has told you that he was certainly in his senses when he cashed it. We have therefore the plea that a man who is sane at ten minutes past one, and sane at fifteen minutes past, may, for the purposes of avoiding the consequences of a crime, call himself insane between those points of time. Really, gentlemen, this is so peculiar a proposition that I am not disposed to weary you with further argument. You will form your own opinion of its value. My friend has adopted this way of saying a great deal to you—and very eloquently— on the score of youth, temptation, and the like. I might point out, however, that the offence with which the prisoner is charged is one of the most serious known to our law; and there are certain features in this case, such as the suspicion which he allowed to rest on his innocent fellow-clerk, and his relations with this married woman, which will render it difficult for you to attach too much importance to such pleading. I ask you, in short, gentlemen, for that verdict of guilty which, in the circumstances, I regard you as, unfortunately, bound to record.

> *Letting his eyes travel from the* JUDGE *and the jury to* FROME, *he sits down.*

THE JUDGE. [*Bending a little towards the jury, and speaking in a business-like voice*] Gentlemen, you have heard the evidence, and the comments on it. My only business is to make clear to you the issues you have to try. The facts are admitted, so far as the alteration of this cheque and counterfoil by the pris-

oner. The defence set up is that he was not in a responsible condition when he committed the crime.
Well, you have heard the prisoner's story, and the
evidence of the other witnesses—so far as it bears on
the point of insanity. If you think that what you have
heard establishes the fact that the prisoner was insane
at the time of the forgery, you will find him guilty,
but insane. If, on the other hand, you conclude from
what you have seen and heard that the prisoner was
sane—and nothing short of insanity will count—you
will find him guilty. In reviewing the testimony as
to his mental condition you must bear in mind very
carefully the evidence as to his demeanour and conduct
both before and after the act of forgery—the evidence
of the prisoner himself, of the woman, of the witness—er
—Cokeson, and—er—of the cashier. And in regard
to that I especially direct your attention to the prisoner's
admission that the idea of adding the t y and the nought
did come into his mind at the moment when the cheque
was handed to him; and also to the alteration of the
counterfoil, and to his subsequent conduct generally.
The bearing of all this on the question of premeditation
(and premeditation will imply sanity) is very obvious.
You must not allow any considerations of age or temptation to weigh with you in the finding of your verdict.
Before you can come to a verdict of guilty but insane
you must be well and thoroughly convinced that the
condition of his mind was such as would have qualified
him at the moment for a lunatic asylum. [*He pauses;
then, seeing that the jury are doubtful whether to retire*

or no, adds:] You may retire, gentlemen, if you wish to do so.

> *The jury retire by a door behind the* JUDGE.
> *The* JUDGE *bends over his notes.* FALDER,
> *leaning from the dock, speaks excitedly to his
> solicitor, pointing down at* RUTH. *The so-
> licitor in turn speaks to* FROME.

FROME. [*Rising*] My lord. The prisoner is very anxious that I should ask you if your lordship would kindly request the reporters not to disclose the name of the woman witness in the Press reports of these proceedings. Your lordship will understand that the consequences might be extremely serious to her.

THE JUDGE. [*Pointedly—with the suspicion of a smile*] Well, Mr. Frome, you deliberately took this course which involved bringing her here.

FROME. [*With an ironic bow*] If your lordship thinks I could have brought out the full facts in any other way?

THE JUDGE. H'm! Well.

FROME. There is very real danger to her, your lordship.

THE JUDGE. You see, I have to take your word for all that.

FROME. If your lordship would be so kind. I can assure your lordship that I am not exaggerating.

THE JUDGE. It goes very much against the grain with me that the name of a witness should ever be suppressed. [*With a glance at* FALDER, *who is gripping and clasping his hands before him, and then at* RUTH, *who is sitting perfectly rigid with her eyes fixed on* FALDER] I'll consider your application.   It must depend.   I have to remember that she may have come here to commit perjury on the prisoner's behalf.

FROME. Your lordship, I really——

THE JUDGE. Yes, yes—I don't suggest anything of the sort, Mr. Frome.   Leave it at that for the moment.

> *As he finishes speaking, the jury return, and file back into the box.*

CLERK OF ASSIZE. Gentlemen, are you agreed on your verdict?

FOREMAN. We are.

CLERK OF ASSIZE.   Is it Guilty, or Guilty but insane?

FOREMAN. Guilty.

> *The* JUDGE *nods; then, gathering up his notes, sits looking at* FALDER, *who stands motionless.*

FROME. [*Rising*] If your lordship would allow me to address you in mitigation of sentence.   I don't know if your lordship thinks I can add anything to what I have said to the jury on the score of the prisoner's youth, and the great stress under which he acted.

THE JUDGE. I don't think you can, Mr. Frome.

FROME. If your lordship says so—I do most earnestly beg your lordship to give the utmost weight to my plea.

> [*He sits down.*

THE JUDGE. [*To the* CLERK] Call upon him.

THE CLERK. Prisoner at the bar, you stand convicted of felony.   Have you anything to say for yourself,

why the Court should not give you judgment according
to law?　　　　　　　　　　[FALDER *shakes his head.*

　　THE JUDGE. William Falder, you have been given
fair trial and found guilty, in my opinion rightly found
guilty, of forgery. [*He pauses; then, consulting his
notes, goes on*] The defence was set up that you were
not responsible for your actions at the moment of
committing this crime. There is no doubt, I think,
that this was a device to bring out at first hand the
nature of the temptation to which you succumbed. For
throughout the trial your counsel was in reality making
an appeal for mercy. The setting up of this defence
of course enabled him to put in some evidence that
might weigh in that direction. Whether he was well
advised to do so is another matter. He claimed that
you should be treated rather as a patient than as a
criminal. And this plea of his, which in the end
amounted to a passionate appeal, he based in effect on
an indictment of the march of Justice, which he prac-
tically accused of confirming and completing the process
of criminality. Now, in considering how far I should
allow weight to his appeal, I have a number of factors
to take into account. I have to consider on the one
hand the grave nature of your offence, the deliberate
way in which you subsequently altered the counterfoil,
the danger you caused to an innocent man—and that,
to my mind, is a very grave point—and finally I have
to consider the necessity of deterring others from following your example. On the other hand, I have to bear
in mind that you are young, that you have hitherto

borne a good character, that you were, if I am to believe
your evidence and that of your witnesses, in a state of
some emotional excitement when you committed this
crime. I have every wish, consistently with my duty—
not only to you, but to the community—to treat you
with leniency. And this brings me to what are the
determining factors in my mind in my consideration
of your case. You are a clerk in a lawyer's office—that
is a very serious element in this case; there can be no
possible excuse made for you on the ground that you
were not fully conversant with the nature of the crime
you were committing, and the penalties that attach to it.
It is said, however, that you were carried away by
your emotions. The story has been told here to-day of
your relations with this—er—Mrs. Honeywill; on that
story both the defence and the plea for mercy were in effect based. Now what is that story? It is that you,
a young man, and she, a young woman, unhappily
married, had formed an attachment, which you both
say—with what truth I am unable to gauge—had not
yet resulted in immoral relations, but which you both
admit was about to result in such relationship. Your
counsel has made an attempt to palliate this, on the
ground that the woman is in what he describes, I
think, as "a hopeless position." As to that I can
express no opinion. She is a married woman, and the
fact is patent that you committed this crime with the
view of furthering an immoral design. Now, however I might wish, I am not able to justify to my con-
science a plea for mercy which has a basis inimical to

morality. It is vitiated *ab initio*, and would, if success-
ful, free you for the completion of this immoral project.
Your counsel has made an attempt to trace your
offence back to what he seems to suggest is a defect in
the marriage law; he has made an attempt also to show
that to punish you with further imprisonment would
be unjust. I do not follow him in these flights. *The
Law is what it is*—a majestic edifice, sheltering all of us,
each stone of which rests on another. I am concerned
only with its administration. The crime you have
committed is a very serious one. I cannot feel it in
accordance with my duty to Society to exercise the pow-
ers I have in your favour. You will go to penal servitude for three years.

> FALDER, *who throughout the* JUDGE'S *speech
> has looked at him steadily, lets his head fall
> forward on his breast.* RUTH *starts up
> from her seat as he is taken out by the warders.
> There is a bustle in court.*

THE JUDGE. [*Speaking to the reporters*] Gentlemen
of the Press, I think that the name of the female witness
should not be reported.

> *The reporters bow their acquiescence.*

THE JUDGE. [*To* RUTH, *who is staring in the direction
in which* FALDER *has disappeared*] Do you understand,
your name will not be mentioned?

COKESON. [*Pulling her sleeve*] The judge is speaking
to you.

> RUTH *turns, stares at the* JUDGE, *and turns
> away.*

THE JUDGE. I shall sit rather late to-day.   Call the next case.

CLERK OF ASSIZE. [*To a warder*] Put up John Booley.

To cries of "Witnesses in the case of Booley":

The curtain falls.

ACT III

SCENE I

A prison. A plainly furnished room, with two large barred windows, overlooking the prisoners' exercise yard, where men, in yellow clothes marked with arrows, and yellow brimless caps, are seen in single file at a distance of four yards from each other, walking rapidly on serpentine white lines marked on the concrete floor of the yard. Two warders in blue uniforms, with peaked caps and swords, are stationed amongst them. The room has distempered walls, a bookcase with numerous official-looking books, a cupboard between the windows, a plan of the prison on the wall, a writing-table covered with documents. It is Christmas Eve.

The GOVERNOR, *a neat, grave-looking man, with a trim, fair moustache, the eyes of a theorist, and grizzled hair, receding from the temples, is standing close to this writing-table looking at a sort of rough saw made out of a piece of metal. The hand in which he holds it is gloved, for two fingers are missing. The chief warder,* WOODER, *a tall, thin, military-*

61

*looking man of sixty, with grey moustache and
melancholy, monkey-like eyes, stands very upright
two paces from him.*

THE GOVERNOR. [*With a faint, abstracted smile*]
Queer-looking affair, Mr. Wooder! Where did you
find it?

WOODER. In his mattress, sir. Haven't come
across such a thing for two years now.

THE GOVERNOR. [*With curiosity*] Had he any set
plan?

WOODER. He'd sawed his window-bar about that
much. [*He holds up his thumb and finger a quarter of
an inch apart*]

THE GOVERNOR. I'll see him this afternoon. What's
his name? Moaney! An old hand, I think?

WOODER. Yes, sir—fourth spell of penal. You'd
think an old lag like him would have had more sense
by now. [*With pitying contempt*] Occupied his mind,
he said. Breaking in and breaking out—that's all
they think about.

THE GOVERNOR. Who's next him?

WOODER. O'Cleary, sir.

THE GOVERNOR. The Irishman.

WOODER. Next him again there's that young fellow,
Falder—star class—and next him old Clipton.

THE GOVERNOR. Ah, yes! "The philosopher." I
want to see him about his eyes.

WOODER. Curious thing, sir: they seem to know
when there's one of these tries at escape going on.

It makes them restive—there's a regular wave going through them just now.

THE GOVERNOR. [*Meditatively*] Odd things—those waves. [*Turning to look at the prisoners exercising*] Seem quiet enough out here!

WOODER. That Irishman, O'Cleary, began banging on his door this morning. Little thing like that's quite enough to upset the whole lot. They're just like dumb animals at times.

THE GOVERNOR. I've seen it with horses before thunder—it'll run right through cavalry lines.

> *The prison* CHAPLAIN *has entered. He is a dark-haired, ascetic man, in clerical undress, with a peculiarly steady, tight-lipped face and slow, cultured speech.*

THE GOVERNOR. [*Holding up the saw*] Seen this, Miller?

THE CHAPLAIN. Useful-looking specimen.

THE GOVERNOR. Do for the Museum, eh! [*He goes to the cupboard and opens it, displaying to view a number of quaint ropes, hooks, and metal tools with labels tied on them*] That'll do, thanks, Mr. Wooder.

WOODER. [*Saluting*] Thank you, sir. [*He goes out.*

THE GOVERNOR. Account for the state of the men last day or two, Miller? Seems going through the whole place.

THE CHAPLAIN. No. I don't know of anything.

THE GOVERNOR. By the way, will you dine with us on Christmas Day?

THE CHAPLAIN. To-morrow. Thanks very much.

THE GOVERNOR. Worries me to feel the men discontented. [*Gazing at the saw*] Have to punish this poor devil. Can't help liking a man who tries to escape. [*He places the saw in his pocket and locks the cupboard again*]

THE CHAPLAIN. Extraordinary perverted will-power—some of them. Nothing to be done till it's broken.

THE GOVERNOR. And not much afterwards, I'm afraid. Ground too hard for golf?

WOODER *comes in again.*

WOODER. Visitor who's been seeing Q 3007 asks to speak to you, sir. I told him it wasn't usual.

THE GOVERNOR. What about?

WOODER. Shall I put him off, sir?

THE GOVERNOR. [*Resignedly*] No, no. Let's see him. Don't go, Miller.

WOODER *motions to some one without, and as the visitor comes in withdraws.*

The visitor is COKESON, *who is attired in a thick overcoat to the knees, woollen gloves, and carries a top hat.*

COKESON. I'm sorry to trouble you. I've been talking to the young man.

THE GOVERNOR. We have a good many here.

COKESON. Name of Falder, forgery. [*Producing a card, and handing it to the* GOVERNOR] Firm of James and Walter How. Well known in the law.

THE GOVERNOR. [*Receiving the card—with a faint smile*] What do you want to see me about, sir?

COKESON. [*Suddenly seeing the prisoners at exercise*] Why! what a sight!

THE GOVERNOR. Yes, we have that privilege from here; my office is being done up. [*Sitting down at his table*] Now, please!

COKESON. [*Dragging his eyes with difficulty from the window*] I *wanted* to say a word to you; I shan't keep you long. [*Confidentially*] Fact is, I oughtn't to be here by rights. His sister came to me—he's got no father and mother—and she was in some distress. "My husband won't let me go and see him," she said; "says he's disgraced the family. And his other sister," she said, "is an invalid." And she asked me to come. Well, I take an interest in him. He was our junior—I go to the same chapel—and I didn't like to refuse. And what I wanted to tell you was, he seems lonely here.

THE GOVERNOR. Not unnaturally.

COKESON. I'm afraid it'll prey on my mind. I see a lot of them about working together.

THE GOVERNOR. Those are local prisoners. The convicts serve their three months here in separate confinement, sir.

COKESON. But we don't want to be unreasonable. He's quite downhearted. I wanted to ask you to let him run about with the others.

THE GOVERNOR. [*With faint amusement*] Ring the bell—would you, Miller? [*To* COKESON] You'd like to hear what the doctor says about him, perhaps.

THE CHAPLAIN. [*Ringing the bell*] You are not accustomed to prisons, it would seem, sir.

COKESON. No. But it's a pitiful sight. He's quite a young fellow. I said to him: "Before a month's up," I said, "you'll be out and about with the others; it'll be a nice change for you." "A month!" he said —like that! "Come!" I said, "we mustn't exaggerate. What's a month? Why, it's nothing!" "A day," he said, "shut up in your cell thinking and brooding as I do, it's longer than a year outside. I can't help it," he said; "I try—but I'm built that way, Mr. Cokeson." And he held his hand up to his face. I could see the tears trickling through his fingers. It wasn't nice.

THE CHAPLAIN. He's a young man with large, rather peculiar eyes, isn't he? Not Church of England, I think?

COKESON. No.

THE CHAPLAIN. I know.

THE GOVERNOR. [*To* WOODER, *who has come in*] Ask the doctor to be good enough to come here for a minute. [WOODER *salutes, and goes out*] Let's see, he's not married?

COKESON. No. [*Confidentially*] But there's a party he's very much attached to, not altogether com-il-fo. It's a sad story.

THE CHAPLAIN. If it wasn't for drink and women, sir, this prison might be closed.

COKESON. [*Looking at the* CHAPLAIN *over his spectacles*] Ye-es, but I wanted to tell you about that, special. He had hopes they'd have let her come

and see him, but they haven't. Of course he asked
me questions. I did my best, but I couldn't tell the
poor young fellow a lie, with him in here—seemed
like hitting him. But I'm afraid it's made him worse.

THE GOVERNOR. What was this news then?

COKESON. Like this. The woman had a nahsty,
spiteful feller for a husband, and she'd left him. Fact
is, she was going away with our young friend. It's
not nice—but I've looked over it. Well, when he was
put in here she said she'd earn her living apart, and
wait for him to come out. That was a great con-
solation to him. But after a month she came to me—
I *don't* know her personally—and she said: "I càn't
earn the children's living, let alone my own—I've got
no friends. I'm obliged to keep out of everybody's
way, else my husband'd get to know where I was. I'm
very much reduced," she said. And she has lost flesh.
"I'll have to go in the workhouse!" It's a painful
story. I said to her: "No," I said, "not that! I've
got a wife an' family, but sooner than you should do
that I'll spare you a little myself." "Really," she
said—she's a nice creature—"I don't like to take it from
you. I think I'd better go back to my husband." Well,
I know he's a nahsty, spiteful feller—drinks—but I
didn't like to persuade her not to.

THE CHAPLAIN. Surely, no.

COKESON. Ye-es, but I'm sorry now; it's upset the
poor young fellow dreadfully. And what I wanted to
say was: He's got his three years to serve. I *want*
things to be pleasant for him.

THE CHAPLAIN. [*With a touch of impatience*] The Law hardly shares your view, I'm afraid.

COKESON. But I can't help thinking that to shut him up there by himself'll turn him silly. And nobody wants that, I s'pose. I *don't* like to see a man cry.

THE CHAPLAIN. It's a very rare thing for them to give way like that.

COKESON. [*Looking at him—in a tone of sudden dogged hostility*] I keep dogs.

THE CHAPLAIN. Indeed?

COKESON. Ye-es. And I say this: I wouldn't shut one of them up all by himself, month after month, not if he'd bit me all over.

THE CHAPLAIN. Unfortunately, the criminal is not a dog; he has a sense of right and wrong.

COKESON. But that's not the way to make him feel it.

THE CHAPLAIN. Ah! there I'm afraid we must differ.

COKESON. It's the same with dogs. If you treat 'em with kindness they'll do anything for you; but to shut 'em up alone, it only makes 'em savage.

THE CHAPLAIN. Surely you should allow those who have had a little more experience than yourself to know what is best for prisoners.

COKESON. [*Doggedly*] I know this young feller, I've watched him for years. He's eurotic—got no stamina. His father died of consumption. I'm thinking of his future. If he's to be kept there shut up by himself, without a cat to keep him company, it'll do him harm. I said to him: "Where do you feel it?" "I can't tell you, Mr. Cokeson," he said, "but sometimes I could beat my head against the wall." It's not nice.

> *During this speech the* DOCTOR *has entered.*
> *He is a medium-sized, rather good-looking*
> *man, with a quick eye. He stands leaning*
> *against the window.*

THE GOVERNOR. This gentleman thinks the separate is telling on Q 3007—Falder, young thin fellow, star class. What do you say, Doctor Clements?

THE DOCTOR. He doesn't like it, but it's not doing him any harm.

COKESON. But he's told me.

THE DOCTOR. Of course he'd say so, but we can always tell. He's lost no weight since he's been here.

COKESON. It's his state of mind I'm speaking of.

THE DOCTOR. His mind's all right so far. He's nervous, rather melancholy. I don't see signs of anything more. I'm watching him carefully.

COKESON. [*Nonplussed*] I'm glad to hear you say that.

THE CHAPLAIN. [*More suavely*] It's just at this period that we are able to make some impression on them, sir. I am speaking from my special standpoint.

COKESON. [*Turning bewildered to the* GOVERNOR] I *don't* want to be unpleasant, but having given him this news, I do feel it's awkward.

THE GOVERNOR. I'll make a point of seeing him to-day.

COKESON. I'm much obliged to you. I thought perhaps seeing him every day you wouldn't notice it.

THE GOVERNOR. [*Rather sharply*] If any sign of injury to his health shows itself his case will be reported at once. That's fully provided for. [*He rises.*

COKESON. [*Following his own thoughts*] Of course, what you don't see doesn't trouble you; but having seen him, I don't want to have him on my mind.

THE GOVERNOR. I think you may safely leave it to us, sir.

COKESON. [*Mollified and apologetic*] I thought you'd understand me. I'm a plain man—never set myself up against authority. [*Expanding to the* CHAPLAIN] Nothing personal meant. *Good*-morning.

> *As he goes out the three officials do not look at each other, but their faces wear peculiar expressions.*

THE CHAPLAIN. Our friend seems to think that prison is a hospital.

COKESON. [*Returning suddenly with an apologetic air*] There's just one little thing. This woman—I suppose I mustn't ask you to let him see her. It'd be a rare treat for them both. He's thinking about her all the time. Of course she's not his wife. But he's quite safe in here. They're a pitiful couple. You couldn't make an exception?

THE GOVERNOR. [*Wearily*] As you say, my dear sir, I couldn't make an exception; he won't be allowed another visit of any sort till he goes to a convict prison.

COKESON. I see. [*Rather coldly*] Sorry to have troubled you.   [*He again goes out.*

THE CHAPLAIN. [*Shrugging his shoulders*] The plain man indeed, poor fellow. Come and have some lunch, Clements?

> *He and the* DOCTOR *go out talking.*
> *The* GOVERNOR, *with a sigh, sits down at his*
> *table and takes up a pen.*
>
> *The curtain falls.*

SCENE II

Part of the ground corridor of the prison. The walls are coloured with greenish distemper up to a stripe of deeper green about the height of a man's shoulder, and above this line are whitewashed. The floor is of blackened stones. Daylight is filtering through a heavily barred window at the end. The doors of four cells are visible. Each cell door has a little round peep-hole at the level of a man's eye, covered by a little round disc, which, raised upwards, affords a view of the cell. On the wall, close to each cell door, hangs a little square board with the prisoner's name, number, and record.

Overhead can be seen the iron structures of the first-floor and second-floor corridors.

The WARDER INSTRUCTOR, *a bearded man in blue uniform, with an apron, and some dangling keys, is just emerging from one of the cells.*

INSTRUCTOR. [*Speaking from the door into the cell*] I'll have another bit for you when that's finished.

O'CLEARY. [*Unseen—in an Irish voice*] Little doubt o' that, sirr.

INSTRUCTOR. [*Gossiping*] Well, you'd rather have it than nothing, I s'pose.

O'CLEARY. An' that's the blessed truth.

> *Sounds are heard of a cell door being closed and locked, and of approaching footsteps.*

INSTRUCTOR. [*In a sharp, changed voice*] Look alive over it!

> *He shuts the cell door, and stands at attention. The* GOVERNOR *comes walking down the corridor, followed by* WOODER.

THE GOVERNOR. Anything to report?

INSTRUCTOR. [*Saluting*] Q 3007 [*he points to a cell*] is behind with his work, sir. He'll lose marks to-day.

> *The* GOVERNOR *nods and passes on to the end cell. The* INSTRUCTOR *goes away.*

THE GOVERNOR. This is our maker of saws, isn't it?

> *He takes the saw from his pocket as* WOODER *throws open the door of the cell. The convict* MOANEY *is seen lying on his bed, athwart the cell, with his cap on. He springs up and stands in the middle of the cell. He is a raw-boned fellow, about fifty-six years old, with outstanding bat's ears and fierce, staring, steel-coloured eyes.*

WOODER. Cap off! [MOANEY *removes his cap*]
Out here!   [MÓANEY *comes to the door.*

THE GOVERNOR. [*Beckoning him out into the corridor, and holding up the saw—with the manner of an
officer speaking to a private*] Anything to say about this,
my man? [MOANEY *is silent*] Come!

MOANEY. It passed the time.

THE GOVERNOR. [*Pointing into the cell*] Not enough
to do, eh?

MOANEY. It don't occupy your mind.

THE GOVERNOR. [*Tapping the saw*] You might find
a better way than this.

MOANEY. [*Sullenly*] Well! What way? I must
keep my hand in against the time I get out. What's
the good of anything else to me at my time of life?
[*With a gradual change to civility, as his tongue warms*]
Ye know that, sir. I'll be in again within a year or
two, after I've done this lot. I don't want to disgrace
meself when I'm out. *You've* got your pride keeping
the prison smart; well, I've got mine. [*Seeing that
the* GOVERNOR *is listening with interest, he goes on,
pointing to the saw*] I *must* be doin' a little o' this.
It's no harm to any one. I was five weeks makin' that
saw—a bit of all right it is, too; now I'll get cells, I
suppose, or seven days' bread and water. You can't
help it, sir, I know that—I quite put meself in your
place.

THE GOVERNOR. Now, look here, Moaney, if I pass
it over will you give me your word not to try it on

again? Think! [*He goes into the cell, walks to the end of it, mounts the stool, and tries the window-bars*]

THE GOVERNOR. [*Returning*] Well?

MOANEY. [*Who has been reflecting*] I've got another six weeks to do in here, alone. I can't do it and think o' nothing. I must have something to interest me. You've made me a sporting offer, sir, but I can't pass my word about it. I shouldn't like to deceive a gentleman. [*Pointing into the cell*] Another four hours' steady work would have done it.

THE GOVERNOR. Yes, and what then? Caught, brought back, punishment. Five weeks' hard work to make this, and cells at the end of it, while they put a new bar to your window. Is it worth it, Moaney?

MOANEY. [*With a sort of fierceness*] Yes, it is.

THE GOVERNOR. [*Putting his hand to his brow*] Oh, well! Two days' cells—bread and water.

MOANEY. Thank 'e, sir.

> *He turns quickly like an animal and slips into his cell.*
>
> *The* GOVERNOR *looks after him and shakes his head as* WOODER *closes and locks the cell door.*

THE GOVERNOR. Open Clipton's cell.

> WOODER *opens the door of* CLIPTON'S *cell.* CLIPTON *is sitting on a stool just inside the door, at work on a pair of trousers. He is a small, thick, oldish man, with an almost shaven head, and smouldering little dark eyes behind smoked spectacles. He gets up*

> *and stands motionless in the doorway, peer-*
> *ing at his visitors.*

THE GOVERNOR. [*Beckoning*] Come out here a minute, Clipton.

> CLIPTON, *with a sort of dreadful quietness,*
> *comes into the corridor, the needle and thread*
> *in his hand. The* GOVERNOR *signs to*
> WOODER, *who goes into the cell and inspects*
> *it carefully.*

THE GOVERNOR. How are your eyes?

CLIPTON. I don't complain of them. I don't see
the sun here. [*He makes a stealthy movement, protruding
his neck a little*] There's just one thing, Mr. Governor,
as you're speaking to me. I wish you'd ask the cove
next door here to keep a bit quieter.

THE GOVERNOR. What's the matter? I don't want
any tales, Clipton.

CLIPTON. He keeps me awake. I don't know who
he is. [*With contempt*] One of this *star* class, I expect.
Oughtn't to be here with *us*.

THE GOVERNOR. [*Quietly*] Quite right, Clipton.
He'll be moved when there's a cell vacant.

CLIPTON. He knocks about like a wild beast in
the early morning. I'm not used to it—stops me
getting my sleep out. In the evening too. It's not
fair, Mr. Governor, as you're speaking to me. Sleep's
the comfort I've got here; I'm entitled to take it out full.

> WOODER *comes out of the cell, and instantly, as*
> *though extinguished,* CLIPTON *moves with*
> *stealthy suddenness back into his cell.*

WOODER. All right, sir.

> *The* GOVERNOR *nods. The door is closed and locked.*

THE GOVERNOR. Which is the man who banged on his door this morning?

WOODER. [*Going towards* O'CLEARY'S *cell*] This one, sir; O'Cleary.

> *He lifts the disc and glances through the peep-hole.*

THE GOVERNOR. Open.

> WOODER *throws open the door.* O'CLEARY, *who is seated at a little table by the door as if listening, springs up and stands at attention just inside the doorway. He is a broad-faced, middle-aged man, with a wide, thin, flexible mouth, and little holes under his high cheek-bones.*

THE GOVERNOR. Where's the joke, O'Cleary?

O'CLEARY. The joke, your honour? I've not seen one for a long time.

THE GOVERNOR. Banging on your door?

O'CLEARY. Oh! that!

THE GOVERNOR. It's womanish.

O'CLEARY. An' it's that I'm becoming this two months past.

THE GOVERNOR. Anything to complain of?

O'CLEARY. No, sirr.

THE GOVERNOR. You're an old hand; you ought to know better.

O'CLEARY. Yes, I've been through it all.

The Governor. You've got a youngster next
door; you'll upset him.

O'Cleary. It cam' over me, your honour. I can't
always be the same steady man.

The Governor. Work all right?

O'Cleary. [*Taking up a rush mat he is making*]
Oh! I can do it on me head. It's the miserablest
stuff—don't take the brains of a mouse. [*Working
his mouth*] It's here I feel it—the want of a little noise—
a terrible little wud ease me.

The Governor. You know as well as I do that if
you were out in the shops you wouldn't be allowed
to talk.

O'Cleary. [*With a look of profound meaning*] Not
with my mouth.

The Governor. Well, then?

O'Cleary. But it's the great conversation I'd have.

The Governor. [*With a smile*] Well, no more
conversation on your door.

O'Cleary. No, sirr, I wud not have the little wit
to repeat meself.

The Governor. [*Turning*] Good-night.

O'Cleary. Good-night, your honour.

> *He turns into his cell.   The* Governor *shuts
> the door.*

The Governor. [*Looking at the record card*] Can't
help liking the poor blackguard.

Wooder. He's an amiable man, sir.

The Governor. [*Pointing down the corridor*] Ask
the doctor to come here, Mr. Wooder.

WOODER *salutes and goes away down the corridor.*

The GOVERNOR *goes to the door of* FALDER'S *cell. He raises his uninjured hand to uncover the peep-hole; but, without uncovering it, shakes his head and drops his hand; then, after scrutinising the record board, he opens the cell door.* FALDER, *who is standing against it, lurches forward.*

THE GOVERNOR. [*Beckoning him out*] Now tell me: can't you settle down, Falder?

FALDER. [*In a breathless voice*] Yes, sir.

THE GOVERNOR. You know what I mean? It's no good running your head against a stone wall, is it?

FALDER. No, sir.

THE GOVERNOR. Well, come.

FALDER. I try, sir.

THE GOVERNOR. Can't you sleep?

FALDER. Very little. Between two o'clock and getting up's the worst time.

THE GOVERNOR. How's that?

FALDER. [*His lips twitch with a sort of smile*] I don't know, sir. I was always nervous. [*Suddenly voluble*] Everything seems to get such a size then. I feel I'll never get out as long as I live.

THE GOVERNOR. That's morbid, my lad. Pull yourself together.

FALDER. [*With an equally sudden dogged resentment*] Yes—I've got to——

THE GOVERNOR. Think of all these other fellows?

FALDER. They're used to it.

THE GOVERNOR. They all had to go through it once for the first time, just as you're doing now.

FALDER. Yes, sir, I shall get to be like them in time, I suppose.

THE GOVERNOR. [*Rather taken aback*] H'm! Well! That rests with you. Now come. Set your mind to it, like a good fellow. You're still quite young. A man can make himself what he likes.

FALDER. [*Wistfully*] Yes, sir.

THE GOVERNOR. Take a good hold of yourself. Do you read?

FALDER. I don't take the words in. [*Hanging his head*] I know it's no good; but I can't help thinking of what's going on outside. In my cell I can't see out at all. It's thick glass, sir.

THE GOVERNOR. You've had a visitor. Bad news?

FALDER. Yes.

THE GOVERNOR. You mustn't think about it.

FALDER. [*Looking back at his cell*] How can I help it, sir?

> *He suddenly becomes motionless as* WOODER
> *and the* DOCTOR *approach. The* GOVERNOR
> *motions to him to go back into his cell.*

FALDER. [*Quick and low*] I'm quite right in my head, sir.   [*He goes back into his cell.*

THE GOVERNOR. [*To the* DOCTOR] Just go in and see him, Clements.

> *The* DOCTOR *goes into the cell. The* GOVER-
> NOR *pushes the door to, nearly closing it, and
> walks towards the window.*

WOODER. [*Following*] Sorry you should be troubled like this, sir. Very contented lot of men, on the whole.

THE GOVERNOR. [*Shortly*] You think so?

WOODER. Yes, sir. It's Christmas doing it, in my opinion.

THE GOVERNOR. [*To himself*] Queer, that!

WOODER. Beg pardon, sir?

THE GOVERNOR. Christmas!

> *He turns towards the window, leaving* WOODER *looking at him with a sort of pained anxiety.*

WOODER. [*Suddenly*] Do you think we make show enough, sir? If you'd like us to have more holly?

THE GOVERNOR. Not at all, Mr. Wooder.

WOODER. Very good, sir.

> *The* DOCTOR *has come out of* FALDER'S *cell, and the* GOVERNOR *beckons to him.*

THE GOVERNOR. Well?

THE DOCTOR. I can't make anything much of him. He's nervous, of course.

THE GOVERNOR. Is there any sort of case to report? Quite frankly, Doctor.

THE DOCTOR. Well, I don't think the separate's doing him any good; but then I could say the same of a lot of them—they'd get on better in the shops, there's no doubt.

THE GOVERNOR. You mean you'd have to recommend others?

THE DOCTOR. A dozen at least. It's on his nerves. There's nothing tangible. That fellow there [*pointing to* O'CLEARY'S *cell*], for instance—feels it just as

much, in his way. If I once get away from physical
facts—I shan't know where I am. Conscientiously,
sir, I don't know how to differentiate him. He hasn't
lost weight. Nothing wrong with his eyes. His pulse
is good. Talks all right.

THE GOVERNOR. It doesn't amount to melancholia?

THE DOCTOR. [*Shaking his head*] I can report on
him if you like; but if I do I ought to report on others.

THE GOVERNOR. I see. [*Looking towards* FALDER'S
cell] The poor devil must just stick it then.

> *As he says this he looks absently at* WOODER.

WOODER. Beg pardon, sir?

> *For answer the* GOVERNOR *stares at him, turns
> on his heel, and walks away.   There is a
> sound as of beating on metal.*

THE GOVERNOR. [*Stopping*] Mr. Wooder?

WOODER. Banging on his door, sir. I thought we
should have more of that.

> *He hurries forward, passing the* GOVERNOR,
> who follows closely.

> *The curtain falls.*

SCENE III

FALDER'S *cell, a whitewashed space thirteen feet broad
by seven deep, and nine feet high, with a rounded
ceiling.   The floor is of shiny blackened bricks.
The barred window of opaque glass, with a ventilator, is high up in the middle of the end wall.   In the*

*middle of the opposite end wall is the narrow door.
In a corner are the mattress and bedding rolled
up (two blankets, two sheets, and a coverlet).   Above
them is a quarter-circular wooden shelf, on which is
a Bible and several little devotional books, piled in
a symmetrical pyramid; there are also a black hair-
brush, tooth-brush, and a bit of soap.   In another
corner is the wooden frame of a bed, standing on
end.   There is a dark ventilator under the window,
and another over the door.   FALDER'S work (a
shirt to which he is putting buttonholes) is hung to a
nail on the wall over a small wooden table, on which
the novel "Lorna Doone" lies open.   Low down
in the corner by the door is a thick glass screen, about
a foot square, covering the gas-jet let into the wall.
There is also a wooden stool, and a pair of shoes
beneath it.   Three bright round tins are set under
the window.*

*In fast-failing daylight, FALDER, in his stockings, is seen
standing motionless, with his head inclined towards
the door, listening.   He moves a little closer to the
door, his stockinged feet making no noise.   He
stops at the door.   He is trying harder and harder
to hear something, any little thing that is going on
outside.   He springs suddenly upright—as if at a
sound—and remains perfectly motionless.   Then,
with a heavy sigh, he moves to his work, and stands
looking at it, with his head down; he does a stitch
or two, having the air of a man so lost in sadness*

that each stitch is, as it were, a coming to life. Then
turning abruptly, he begins pacing the cell, moving
his head, like an animal pacing its cage. He stops
again at the door, listens, and, placing the palms of
his hands against it with his fingers spread out, leans
his forehead against the iron. Turning from it,
presently, he moves slowly back towards the window,
tracing his way with his finger along the top line
of the distemper that runs round the wall. He
stops under the window, and, picking up the lid of
one of the tins, peers into it. It has grown very
nearly dark. Suddenly the lid falls out of his hand
with a clatter—the only sound that has broken the
silence—and he stands staring intently at the wall
where the stuff of the shirt is hanging rather white
in the darkness—he seems to be seeing somebody or
something there. There is a sharp tap and click;
the cell light behind the glass screen has been turned
up. The cell is brightly lighted. FALDER *is seen*
gasping for breath.

A sound from far away, as of distant, dull beating on
thick metal, is suddenly audible. FALDER *shrinks*
back, not able to bear this sudden clamour. But the
sound grows, as though some great tumbril were
rolling towards the cell. And gradually it seems to
hypnotise him. He begins creeping inch by inch
nearer to the door. The banging sound, travelling
from cell to cell, draws closer and closer; FALDER'S
hands are seen moving as if his spirit had already

joined in this beating, and the sound swells till it seems to have entered the very cell. He suddenly raises his clenched fists. Panting violently, he flings himself at his door. and beats on it.

The curtain falls.

ACT IV

The scene is again COKESON'S *room, at a few minutes to
ten of a March morning, two years later. The doors
are all open.* SWEEDLE, *now blessed with a sprout-
ing moustache, is getting the offices ready. He
arranges papers on* COKESON'S *table; then goes to a
covered washstand, raises the lid, and looks at himself in the mirror. While he is gazing his fill*
RUTH HONEYWILL *comes in through the outer
office and stands in the doorway. There seems a
kind of exultation and excitement behind her ha-
bitual impassivity.*

SWEEDLE. [*Suddenly seeing her, and dropping the
lid of the washstand with a bang*] Hello! It's you!

RUTH. Yes.

SWEEDLE. There's only me here! They don't
waste their time hurrying down in the morning. Why,
it must be two years since we had the pleasure of seeing
you. [*Nervously*] What have you been doing with
yourself?

RUTH. [*Sardonically*] Living.

SWEEDLE. [*Impressed*] If you want to see *him*
[*he points to* COKESON'S *chair*], he'll be here directly
—never misses—not much. [*Delicately*] I hope our

friend's back from the country. His time's been up
these three months, if I remember. [RUTH *nods*] I
was awful sorry about that. The governor made a
mistake—if you ask me.

RUTH. He did.

SWEEDLE. He ought to have given him a chanst.
And, *I* say, the judge ought to ha' let him go after that.
They've forgot what human nature's like. Whereas
we know.   RUTH *gives him a honeyed smile.*

SWEEDLE. They come down on you like a cartload
of bricks, flatten you out, and when you don't swell
up again they complain of it. I know 'em—seen a
lot of that sort of thing in my time. [*He shakes his
head in the plenitude of wisdom*] Why, only the other
day the governor——

> *But* COKESON *has come in through the outer
> office; brisk with east wind, and decidedly
> greyer.*

COKESON. [*Drawing off his coat and gloves*] Why!
it's you! [*Then motioning* SWEEDLE *out, and closing
the door*] Quite a stranger! Must be two years.
D'you want to see me? I can give you a minute.
Sit down! Family well?

RUTH. Yes. I'm not living where I was.

COKESON. [*Eyeing her askance*] I hope things are
more comfortable at home.

RUTH. I couldn't stay with Honeywill, after all.

COKESON. You haven't done anything rash, I hope.
I should be sorry if you'd done anything rash.

RUTH. I've kept the children with me.

COKESON. [*Beginning to feel that things are not so jolly as he had hoped*] Well, I'm glad to have seen you. You've not heard from the young man, I suppose, since he came out?

RUTH. Yes, I ran across him yesterday.

COKESON. I hope he's well.

RUTH. [*With sudden fierceness*] He can't get anything to do. It's dreadful to see him. He's just skin and bone.

COKESON. [*With genuine concern*] Dear me! I'm sorry to hear that. [*On his guard again*] Didn't they find him a place when his time was up?

RUTH. He was only there three weeks. It got out.

COKESON. I'm sure I don't know what I can do for you. I don't like to be snubby.

RUTH. I can't bear his being like that.

COKESON. [*Scanning her not unprosperous figure*] I know his relations aren't very forthy about him. Perhaps *you* can do something for him, till he finds his feet.

RUTH. Not now. I could have—but not *now*.

COKESON. I don't understand.

RUTH. [*Proudly*] I've seen him again—that's all over.

COKESON. [*Staring at her—disturbed*] I'm a family man—I don't want to hear anything unpleasant. Excuse me—I'm very busy.

RUTH. I'd have gone home to my people in the country long ago, but they've never got over me marrying Honeywill. I never was waywise, Mr. Cokeson, but I'm proud. I was only a girl, you see, when I married him. I thought the world of him, of course . . . he used to come travelling to our farm.

COKESON. [*Regretfully*] I did hope you'd have got on better, after you saw me.

RUTH. He used me worse than ever. He couldn't break my nerve, but I lost my health; and then he began knocking the children about. . . . I couldn't stand that. I wouldn't go back now, if he were dying.

COKESON. [*Who has risen and is shifting about as though dodging a stream of lava*] We mustn't be violent, must we?

RUTH. [*Smouldering*] A man that can't behave better than that—— [*There is silence.*

COKESON. [*Fascinated in spite of himself*] Then there you were! And what did you do then?

RUTH. [*With a shrug*] Tried the same as when I left him before . . . making skirts . . . cheap things. It was the best I could get, but I never made more than ten shillings a week, buying my own cotton and working all day; I hardly ever got to bed till past twelve. I kept at it for nine months. [*Fiercely*] Well, I'm not fit for that; I wasn't made for it. I'd rather die.

COKESON. My dear woman! We mustn't talk like that.

RUTH. It was starvation for the children too—after what they'd always had. I soon got not to care. I used to be too tired. [*She is silent.*

COKESON. [*With fearful curiosity*] Why, what happened then?

RUTH. [*With a laugh*] My employer happened then—he's happened ever since.

COKESON. Dear! Oh dear! I never came across a thing like this.

RUTH. [*Dully*] He's treated me all right. But I've done with that. [*Suddenly her lips begin to quiver, and she hides them with the back of her hand*] I never thought I'd see *him* again, you see. It was just a chance I met him by Hyde Park. We went in there and sat down, and he told me all about himself. Oh! Mr. Cokeson, give him another chance.

COKESON. [*Greatly disturbed*] Then you've both lost your livings! What a horrible position!

RUTH. If he could only get here—where there's nothing to find out about him!

COKESON. We can't have anything derogative to the firm.

RUTH. I've no one else to go to.

COKESON. I'll speak to the partners, but I don't think they'll take him, under the circumstances. I don't really.

RUTH. He came with me; he's down there in the street.   [*She points to the window.*

COKESON. [*On his dignity*] He shouldn't have done that until he's sent for. [*Then softening at the look on her face*] We've got a vacancy, as it happens, but I can't promise anything.

RUTH. It would be the saving of him.

COKESON. Well, I'll do what I can, but I'm not sanguine. Now tell him that I don't want him till I see how things are. Leave your address? [*Repeating her*] 83 Mullingar Street? [*He notes it on blotting-paper*] Good-morning.

RUTH. Thank you.

> *She moves towards the door, turns as if to speak, but does not, and goes away.*

COKESON. [*Wiping his head and forehead with a large white cotton handkerchief*] What a business! *Then looking amongst his papers, he sounds his bell.* SWEEDLE *answers it*]

COKESON. Was that young Richards coming here to-day after the clerk's place?

SWEEDLE. Yes.

COKESON. Well, keep him in the air; I don't want to see him yet.

SWEEDLE. What shall I tell him, sir?

COKESON. [*With asperity*] Invent something. Use your brains. Don't stump him off altogether.

SWEEDLE. Shall I tell him that we've got illness, sir?

COKESON. No! Nothing untrue. Say I'm not here to-day.

SWEEDLE. Yes, sir. Keep him hankering?

COKESON. Exactly. And look here. You remember Falder? I may be having him round to see me. Now, treat him like you'd have him treat you in a similar position.

SWEEDLE. I naturally should do.

COKESON. That's right. When a man's down never hit 'im. 'Tisn't necessary. Give him a hand up. That's a metaphor I recommend to you in life. It's sound policy.

SWEEDLE. Do you think the governors will take him on again, sir?

COKESON. Can't say anything about that. [*At the sound of some one having entered the outer office*] Who's there?

SWEEDLE. [*Going to the door and looking*] It's Falder, sir.

COKESON. [*Vexed*] Dear me! That's very naughty of her. Tell him to call again. I don't want——

> *He breaks off as* FALDER *comes in.* FALDER *is thin, pale, older, his eyes have grown more restless. His clothes are very worn and loose.*
>
> SWEEDLE, *nodding cheerfully, withdraws.*

COKESON. Glad to see you. You're rather previous. [*Trying to keep things pleasant*] Shake hands! She's striking while the iron's hot. [*He wipes his forehead*] I don't blame her. She's anxious.

> FALDER *timidly takes* COKESON's *hand and glances towards the partners' door.*

COKESON. No—not yet! Sit down! [FALDER *sits in the chair at the side of* COKESON's *table, on which he places his cap*] Now you are here I'd like you to give me a little account of yourself. [*Looking at him over his spectacles*] How's your health?

FALDER I'm alive. Mr. Cokeson.

COKESON. [*Preoccupied*] I'm glad to hear that. About this matter. I don't like doing anything out of the ordinary; it's not my habit. I'm a plain man, and I want everything smooth and straight. But I promised your friend to speak to the partners, and I always keep my word.

FALDER. I just want a chance, Mr. Cokeson. I've paid for that job a thousand times and more. I have, sir. No one knows. They say I weighed more when I came out than when I went in. They couldn't weigh me here [*he touches his head*] or here [*he touches his heart, and gives a sort of laugh*]. Till last night I'd have thought there was nothing in here at all.

COKESON. [*Concerned*] You've not got heart disease?

FALDER. Oh! they passed me sound enough.

COKESON. But they got you a place, didn't they?

FALDER. Yes; very good people, knew all about it—very kind to me. I thought I was going to get on first rate. But one day, all of a sudden, the other clerks got wind of it. . . . I couldn't stick it, Mr. Cokeson, I couldn't, sir.

COKESON. Easy, my dear fellow, easy!

FALDER. I had one small job after that, but it didn't last.

COKESON. How was that?

FALDER. It's no good deceiving you, Mr. Cokeson. The fact is, I seem to be struggling against a thing that's all round me. I can't explain it: it's as if I was in a net; as fast as I cut it here, it grows up there.

I didn't act as I ought to have, about references; but what are you to do? You must have them. And that made me afraid, and I left. In fact, I'm—I'm afraid all the time now.

> *He bows his head and leans dejectedly silent over the table.*

COKESON. I feel for you—I do really. Aren't your sisters going to do anything for you?

FALDER. One's in consumption. And the other——

COKESON. Ye . . . es. She told me her husband wasn't quite pleased with you.

FALDER. When I went there—they were at supper—my sister wanted to give me a kiss—I know. But he just looked at her, and said: "What have you come for?" Well, I pocketed my pride and I said: "Aren't you going to give me your hand, Jim? Cis is, I know," I said. "Look here!" he said, "that's all very well, but we'd better come to an understanding. I've been expecting you, and I've made up my mind. I'll give you fifteen pounds to go to Canada with." "I see," I said—"good riddance! No, thanks; keep your fifteen pounds." Friendship's a queer thing when you've been where I have.

COKESON. I understand. Will you take the fifteen pound from me? [*Flustered, as* FALDER *regards him with a queer smile*] Quite without prejudice; I meant it kindly.

FALDER. I'm not allowed to leave the country.

COKESON. Oh! ye . . . es—ticket-of-leave? You aren't looking the thing.

FALDER. I've slept in the Park three nights this week. The dawns aren't all poetry there. But meeting her—I feel a different man this morning. I've often thought the being fond of her's the best thing about me; it's sacred, somehow—and yet it did for me. That's queer, isn't it?

COKESON. I'm sure we're all very sorry for you.

FALDER. That's what I've found, Mr. Cokeson. Awfully sorry for me. [*With quiet bitterness*] But it doesn't do to associate with criminals!

COKESON. Come, come, it's no use calling yourself names. That never did a man any good. Put a face on it.

FALDER. It's easy enough to put a face on it, sir, when you're independent. Try it when you're down like me. They talk about giving you your deserts. Well, I think I've had just a bit over.

COKESON. [*Eyeing him askance over his spectacles*] I hope they haven't made a Socialist of you.

> FALDER *is suddenly still, as if brooding over*
> *his past self; he utters a peculiar laugh.*

COKESON. You must give them credit for the best intentions. Really you must. Nobody wishes you harm, I'm sure.

FALDER. I believe that, Mr. Cokeson. Nobody wishes you harm, but they down you all the same. This feeling—— [*He stares round him, as though at something closing in*] It's crushing me. [*With sudden impersonality*] I know it is.

COKESON. [*Horribly disturbed*] There's nothing there!

We must try and take it quiet. I'm sure I've often
had you in my prayers. Now leave it to me. I'll use
my gumption and take 'em when they're jolly.

> [*As he speaks the two partners come in.*

COKESON. [*Rather disconcerted, but trying to put
them all at ease*] I didn't expect you quite so soon. I've
just been having a talk with this young man. I think
you'll remember him.

JAMES. [*With a grave, keen look*] Quite well. How
are you, Falder?

WALTER. [*Holding out his hand almost timidly*]
Very glad to see you again, Falder.

FALDER. [*Who has recovered his self-control, takes
the hand*] Thank you, sir.

COKESON. Just a word, Mr. James. [*To* FALDER,
pointing to the clerks' office] You might go in there a
minute. You know your way. Our junior won't be
coming this morning. His wife's just had a little
family.

> FALDER *goes uncertainly out into the clerks' office.*

COKESON. [*Confidentially*] I'm bound to tell you all
about it. He's quite penitent. But there's a prejudice against him. And you're not seeing him to
advantage this morning; he's under-nourished. It's
very trying to go without your dinner.

JAMES. Is that so, Cokeson?

COKESON. I wanted to ask you. He's had his lesson.
Now *we* know all about him, and we want a clerk.
There is a young fellow applying, but I'm keeping
him in the air.

JAMES. A gaol-bird in the office, Cokeson? J don't see it.

WALTER. "The rolling of the chariot-wheels of Justice!" I've never got that out of my head.

JAMES. I've nothing to reproach myself with in this affair. What's he been doing since he came out?

COKESON. He's had one or two places, but he hasn't kept them. He's ser itive—quite natural. Seems to fancy everybody's dow ı on him.

JAMES. Bad sign. Don't like the fellow—never did from the first. "Weak character" 's written all over him.

WALTER. I think we owe him a leg up.

JAMES. He brought it all on himself.

WALTER. The doctrine of full responsibility doesn't quite hold in these days.

JAMES. [*Rather grimly*] You'll find it safer to hold it for all that, my boy.

WALTER. For oneself, yes—not for other people, thanks.

JAMES. Well! I don't want to be hard.

COKESON. I'm glad to hear you say that. He seems to see something [*spreading his arms*] round him. 'Tisn't healthy.

JAMES. What about that woman he was mixed up with? I saw some one uncommonly like her outside as we came in.

COKESON. *That!* Well, I can't keep anything from you. He has met her.

JAMES. Is she with her husband?

COKESON. No.

JAMES. Falder living with her, I suppose?

COKESON. [*Desperately trying to retain the new-found jollity*] I don't know that of my own knowledge. 'Tisn't my business.

JAMES. It's *our* business, if we're going to engage him, Cokeson.

COKESON. [*Reluctantly*] I ought to tell you, perhaps. I've had the party here this morning.

JAMES. I thought so. [*To* WALTER] No, my dear boy, it won't do. Too shady altogether!

COKESON. The two things together make it very awkward for you—I see that.

WALTER. [*Tentatively*] I don't quite know what we have to do with his private life.

JAMES. No, no! He must make a clean sheet of it, or he can't come here.

WALTER. Poor devil!

COKESON. Will you have him in? [*And as* JAMES *nods*] I think I can get him to see reason.

JAMES. [*Grimly*] You can leave that to me, Cokeson.

WALTER. [*To* JAMES, *in a low voice, while* COKESON *is summoning* FALDER] His whole future may depend on what we do, dad.

> FALDER *comes in. He has pulled himself together, and presents a steady front.*

JAMES. Now look here, Falder. My son and I want to give you another chance; but there are two things I must say to you. In the first place: It's no good coming here as a victim. If you've any notion that

you've been unjustly treated—get rid of it. You can't
play fast and loose with morality and hope to go scot-
free. If Society didn't take care of itself, nobody
would—the sooner you realise that the better.

FALDER. Yes, sir; but—may I say something?

JAMES. Well?

FALDER. I had a lot of time to think it over in
prison.   [*He stops.*

COKESON. [*Encouraging him*] I'm sure you did.

FALDER. There were all sorts there. And what I
mean, sir, is, that if we'd been treated differently the first
time, and put under somebody that could look after us a
bit, and not put in prison, not a quarter of us would
ever have got there.

JAMES. [*Shaking his head*] I'm afraid I've very
grave doubts of that, Falder.

FALDER. [*With a gleam of malice*] Yes, sir, so I found.

JAMES. My good fellow, don't forget that you began it.

FALDER. I never wanted to do wrong.

JAMES. Perhaps not. But you did.

FALDER. [*With all the bitterness of his past suffering*]
It's knocked me out of time. [*Pulling himself up*]
That is, I mean, I'm not what I was.

JAMES. This isn't encouraging for us, Falder.

COKESON. He's putting it awkwardly, Mr. James.

FALDER. [*Throwing over his caution from the intensity of his feeling*] I mean it, Mr. Cokeson.

JAMES. Now, lay aside all those thoughts, Falder,
and look to the future.

FALDER. [*Almost eagerly*] Yes, sir, but you don't understand what prison is.   It's here it gets you.

> *He grips his chest.*

COKESON. [*In a whisper to* JAMES] I told you he wanted nourishment.

WALTER. Yes, but, my dear fellow, that'll pass away.   Time's merciful.

FALDER. [*With his face twitching*] I hope so, sir.

JAMES. [*Much more gently*] Now, my boy, what you've got to do is to put all the past behind you and build yourself up a steady reputation.   And that brings me to the second thing.   This woman you were mixed up with—you must give us your word, you know, to have done with that.   There's no chance of your keeping straight if you're going to begin your future with such a relationship.

FALDER. [*Looking from one to the other with a hunted expression*] But sir . . . but sir . . . it's the one thing I looked forward to all that time.   And she too . . . I couldn't find her before last night.

> *During this and what follows* COKESON *becomes more and more uneasy.*

JAMES. This is painful, Falder.   But you must see for yourself that it's impossible for a firm like this to close its eyes to everything.   Give us this proof of your resolve to keep straight, and you can come back—not otherwise.

FALDER. [*After staring at* JAMES, *suddenly stiffens himself*] I couldn't give her up.   I couldn't!   Oh, sir!

I'm all she's got to look to.   And I'm sure she's all I've got.

JAMES. I'm very sorry, Falder, but I must be firm. It's for the benefit of you both in the long run.   No good can come of this connection.   It was the cause of all your disaster.

FALDER. But sir, it means—having gone through all that—getting broken up—my nerves are in an awful state—for nothing.   I did it for her.

JAMES. Come! If she's anything of a woman she'll see it for herself.   She won't want to drag you down further.   If there were a prospect of your being able to marry her—it might be another thing.

FALDER. It's not my fault, sir, that she couldn't get rid of him—she would have if she could.   That's been the whole trouble from the beginning.   [*Looking suddenly at* WALTER] . . . If anybody would help her! It's only money wanted now, I'm sure.

COKESON. [*Breaking in, as* WALTER *hesitates, and is about to speak*] I don't think we need consider that —it's rather far-fetched.

FALDER. [*To* WALTER, *appealing*] He must have given her full cause since; she could prove that he drove her to leave him.

WALTER. I'm inclined to do what you say, Falder, if it can be managed.

FALDER. Oh, sir !

> *He goes to the window and looks down into the street.*

COKESON. [*Hurriedly*] You don't take me, Mr. Walter. I have my reasons.

FALDER. [*From the window*] She's down there, sir. Will you see her? I can beckon to her from here.

> WALTER *hesitates, and looks from* COKESON *to* JAMES.

JAMES. [*With a sharp nod*] Yes, let her come.

> FALDER *beckons from the window.*

COKESON. [*In a low fluster to* JAMES *and* WALTER] No, Mr. James. She's not been quite what she ought to ha' been, while this young man's been away. She's lost her chance. We can't consult how to swindle the Law.

> FALDER *has come from the window. The three men look at him in a sort of awed silence.*

FALDER. [*With instinctive apprehension of some change—looking from one to the other*] There's been nothing between us, sir, to prevent it. . . . What I said at the trial was true. And last night we only just sat in the Park.

> SWEEDLE *comes in from the outer office.*

COKESON. What is it?

SWEEDLE. Mrs. Honeywill.   [*There is silence.*

JAMES. Show her in.

> RUTH *comes slowly in, and stands stoically with* FALDER *on one side and the three men on the other. No one speaks.* COKE-SON *turns to his table, bending over his*

> *papers as though the burden of the situation were forcing him back into his accustomed groove.*

JAMES. [*Sharply*] Shut the door there. [SWEEDLE *shuts the door*] We've asked you to come up because there are certain facts to be faced in this matter. I understand you have only just met Falder again.

RUTH. Yes—only yesterday.

JAMES. He's told us about himself, and we're very sorry for him. I've promised to take him back here if he'll make a fresh start. [*Looking steadily at* RUTH] This is a matter that requires courage, ma'am.

> RUTH, *who is looking at* FALDER, *begins to twist her hands in front of her as though prescient of disaster.*

FALDER. Mr. Walter How is good enough to say that he'll help us to get you a divorce.

> RUTH *flashes a startled glance at* JAMES *and* WALTER.

JAMES. I don't think that's practicable, Falder.

FALDER. But, sir——!

JAMES. [*Steadily*] Now, Mrs. Honeywill. You're fond of him.

RUTH. Yes, sir; I love him.

> *She looks miserably at* FALDER.

JAMES. Then you don't want to stand in his way, do you?

RUTH. [*In a faint voice*] I could take care of him.

JAMES. The best way you can take care of him will be to give him up.

FALDER. Nothing shall make me give you up. You can get a divorce. There's been nothing between us, has there?

RUTH. [*Mournfully shaking her head—without looking at him*] No.

FALDER. We'll keep apart till it's over, sir; if you'll only help us—we promise.

JAMES. [*To* RUTH] You see the thing plainly, don't you? You see what I mean?

RUTH. [*Just above a whisper*] Yes.

COKESON. [*To himself*] There's a dear woman.

JAMES. The situation is impossible.

RUTH. Must I, sir?

JAMES. [*Forcing himself to look at her*] I put it to you, ma'am. His future is in your hands.

RUTH. [*Miserably*] I want to do the best for him.

JAMES. [*A little huskily*] That's right, that's right!

FALDER. I don't understand. You're not going to give me up—after all this? There's something—— [*Starting forward to* JAMES] Sir, I swear solemnly there's been nothing between us.

JAMES. I believe you, Falder. Come, my lad, be as plucky as she is.

FALDER. Just now you were going to help us. [*He stares at* RUTH, *who is standing absolutely still; his face and hands twitch and quiver as the truth dawns on him*] What is it? You've not been——

WALTER. Father!

JAMES. [*Hurriedly*] There, there! That'll do, that'll

do! I'll give you your chance, Falder. Don't let me
know what you do with yourselves, that's all.

FALDER. [*As if he has not heard*] Ruth?

> RUTH *looks at him; and* FALDER *covers his face
> with his hands. There is silence.*

COKESON. [*Suddenly*] There's some one out there.
[*To* RUTH] Go in here. You'll feel better by yourself
for a minute.

> *He points to the clerks' room and moves tow-
> ards the outer office.* FALDER *does not move.*
> RUTH *puts out her hand timidly. He
> shrinks back from the touch. She turns
> and goes miserably into the clerks' room.
> With a brusque movement he follows, seiz-
> ing her by the shoulder just inside the door-
> way.* COKESON *shuts the door.*

JAMES. [*Pointing to the outer office*] Get rid of that,
whoever it is.

SWEEDLE. [*Opening the office door, in a scared voice*]
Detective-Sergeant Wister.

> *The detective enters, and closes the door behind
> him.*

WISTER. Sorry to disturb you, sir. A clerk you
had here, two years and a half ago. I arrested him
in this room.

JAMES. What about him?

WISTER. I thought perhaps I might get his where-
abouts from you. [*There is an awkward silence.*

COKESON. [*Pleasantly, coming to the rescue*] We're
not responsible for his movements; you know that.

JAMES. What do you want with him?

WISTER. He's failed to report himself this last four weeks.

WALTER. How d'you mean?

WISTER. Ticket-of-leave won't be up for another six months, sir.

WALTER. Has he to keep in touch with the police till then?

WISTER. We're bound to know where he sleeps every night. I dare say we shouldn't interfere, sir, even though he hasn't reported himself. But we've just heard there's a serious matter of obtaining employment with a forged reference. What with the two things together—we must have him.

> *Again there is silence.* WALTER *and* COKESON
> *steal glances at* JAMES, *who stands staring
> steadily at the detective.*

COKESON. [*Expansively*] We're very busy at the moment. If you could make it convenient to call again we might be able to tell you then.

JAMES. [*Decisively*] I'm a servant of the Law, but I dislike peaching. In fact, I can't do such a thing. If you want him you must find him without us.

> *As he speaks his eye falls on* FALDER'S *cap,
> still lying on the table, and his face contracts.*

WISTER. [*Noting the gesture—quietly*] Very good, sir. I ought to warn you that, having broken the terms of his licence, he's still a convict, and sheltering a convict——

JAMES. I shelter no one. But you mustn't come here and ask questions which it's not my business to answer.

WISTER. [*Dryly*] I won't trouble you further then, gentlemen.

COKESON. I'm sorry we couldn't give you the information. You quite understand, don't you? Good-morning!

> WISTER *turns to go, but instead of going to the door of the outer office he goes to the door of the clerks' room.*

COKESON. The other door . . . the other door!

> WISTER *opens the clerks' door.* RUTH's *voice is heard:* "*Oh, do!*" *and* FALDER's: "*I can't!*" *There is a little pause; then, with sharp fright,* RUTH *says:* "*Who's that?*" WISTER *has gone in.*

> *The three men look aghast at the door.*

WISTER. [*From within*] Keep back, please!

> *He comes swiftly out with his arm twisted in* FALDER's. *The latter gives a white, staring look at the three men.*

WALTER. Let him go this time, for God's sake!

WISTER. I couldn't take the responsibility, sir.

FALDER. [*With a queer, desperate laugh*] Good!

> *Flinging a look back at* RUTH, *he throws up his head, and goes out through the outer office, half dragging* WISTER *after him.*

WALTER. [*With despair*] That finishes him. It'll go on for ever now.

> SWEEDLE *can be seen staring through the outer door. There are sounds of footsteps descending the stone stairs; suddenly a dull thud, a faint "My God!" in* WISTER'S *voice.*

JAMES. What's that?

> SWEEDLE *dashes forward. The door swings to behind him. There is dead silence.*

WALTER. [*Starting forward to the inner room*] The woman—she's fainting!

> *He and* COKESON *support the fainting* RUTH *from the doorway of the clerks' room.*

COKESON. [*Distracted*] Here, my dear! There, there!

WALTER. Have you any brandy?

COKESON. I've got sherry.

WALTER. Get it, then. Quick!

> *He places* RUTH *in a chair—which* JAMES *has dragged forward.*

COKESON. [*With sherry*] Here! It's good strong sherry. [*They try to force the sherry between her lips. There is the sound of feet, and they siop to listen.*

> *The outer door is reopened—*WISTER *and* SWEEDLE *are seen carrying some burden.*

JAMES. [*Hurrying forward*] What is it?

> *They lay the burden down in the outer office, out of sight, and all but* RUTH *cluster round it, speaking in hushed voices.*

WISTER. He jumped—neck's broken.

WALTER. Good God!

WISTER. He must have been mad to think he could give me the slip like that. And what was it—just a few months!

WALTER. [*Bitterly*] Was that all?

JAMES. What a desperate thing! [*Then, in a voice unlike his own*] Run for a doctor—you! [SWEEDLE *rushes from the outeroffice*] An ambulance!

> WISTER *goes out. On* RUTH'S *face an expression of fear and horror has been seen growing, as if she dared not turn towards the voices. She now rises and steals towards them.*

WALTER. [*Turning suddenly*] Look!

> *The three men shrink back out of her way, one by one, into* COKESON'S *room.* RUTH *drops on her knees by the body.*

RUTH. [*In a whisper*] What is it? He's not breathing. [*She crouches over him*] My dear! My pretty!

> *In the outer office doorway the figures of men are seen standing.*

RUTH. [*Leaping to her feet*] No, no! No, no! He's dead!   [*The figures of the men shrink back.*

COKESON. [*Stealing forward. In a hoarse voice*] There, there, poor dear woman!

> *At the sound behind her* RUTH *faces round at him.*

COKESON. No one'll touch him now!   Never again!
He's safe with gentle Jesus!

> RUTH *stands as though turned to stone in the
> doorway staring at* COKESON, *who, bending
> humbly before her, holds out his hand as one
> would to a lost dog.*

> *The curtain falls.*

Printed in the United States
1487400001B/61

9 781589 634664